# Oxfc

# Children's
# Maths
## and
# Science
## Words

**Compiled by**
Peter Patilla and
Graham Peacock

**Illustrated by**
Georgie Birkett and
David Semple

OXFORD
UNIVERSITY PRESS

## My name is

. . . . . . . . . . . . . . . . . . . . . . . . . . . . . . . . . . . . . . . . . . . . . . . . . . . . . . .

**OXFORD**
UNIVERSITY PRESS

Great Clarendon Street, Oxford OX2 6DP
Oxford University Press is a department of the University of Oxford.
It furthers the University's objective of excellence in research, scholarship,
and education by publishing worldwide.

Oxford is a registered trade mark of Oxford University Press
in the UK and in certain other countries

First published 2021

Adapted from Oxford First Illustrated Maths Dictionary, 2001
and Oxford First Illustrated Science Dictionary, 2003

Database right Oxford University Press (maker)

British Library Cataloguing in Publication Data available

ISBN 978-0-19-277792-8

1 3 5 7 9 10 8 6 4 2

Printed in China

Paper used in the production of this book is a natural,
recyclable product made from wood grown in sustainable forests.
The manufacturing process conforms to the environmental regulations
of the country of origin.

**Oxford OWL**

**For school**
Discover eBooks, inspirational resources, advice and support

**For home**
Helping your child's learning with free eBooks, essential tips and fun activities

**www.oxfordowl.co.uk**

**Oxford Corpus**

You can trust this book to be up to date, relevant and engaging because it is powered by the Oxford Corpus, a unique living database of children's and adults' language.

**Acknowledgements**
The publisher and authors would like to thank
the following for permission to use photographs
and other copyright material:

All photos © Shutterstock
Artwork by Georgie Birkett, David Semple,
Dynamo, and Oxford University Press (UK & ANZ)

The publishers would like to thank Jill Jesson for
her contribution to this edition.

Every effort has been made to contact copyright
holders of material reproduced in this book.
Any omissions will be rectified in subsequent
printings if notice is given to the publisher.

# Contents

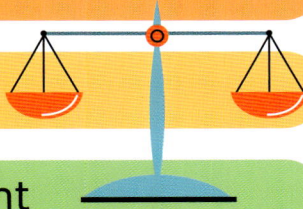

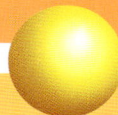

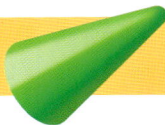

# Introduction

*Oxford Children's Maths and Science Words* contains over 600 scientific, mathematical and computing words in alphabetical order, each with a simple meaning. Colourful pictures and diagrams support the text, while example sentences and labels expand or further explain the word.

The words in this dictionary have been carefully chosen to help children develop their scientific, mathematical and computing language and understanding. At the end of this book, there are lists of doing words and additional information on equipment, dates,

**beginning letter**

**word**

**meaning or definition**

**position of letter in the alphabet**

**different meanings of the same word**

**page numbers for related words to help expand vocabulary**

A B C D E F G H I J K **Ll** M N O P Q R S T U V W X Y Z

## living
Something that is living is alive.

## lizard
A lizard is an animal with a long body, four legs and a long tail. Lizards are reptiles.

## log
❶ A log is a part of a tree that has been chopped down. You can burn logs on a fire.

❷ When you log in to a computer, you switch it on so that you can use it. When you log out, you shut it down and switch it off.

*You might need your username and password to **log** in.*

Log in
username
password
Log in

Look up the word *password* on page 72.

## logic
Logic is an organized way of thinking and working things out.

*You use **logic** to complete a puzzle.*

## long
Long describes the length of something.

*You place things side by side to find the **longest**.*

long
longer
longest

## loud
Something loud is easy to hear.

*Suddenly, there was a **loud** bang.*

## lungs
Many animals breathe air through lungs. Some tiny animals, such as insects, do not have lungs.

lungs

numbers, times tables and shapes that children are likely to use in their maths, science and computing lessons. The dictionary will also teach children how to locate a word using its first letter, and how to interpret information from words, pictures and diagrams.

Finally it will foster children's natural curiosity about numbers, technology and the world around them.

**capital letter**

**small letter**

# Mm

is for **mole**

**male**
A male animal does not give birth or lay eggs.

*A cockerel is a **male** chicken.*

**meaning given in a sentence**

**machine**
Machines help us do work.

**mammal**
Mammals are furry or hairy animals. Mammal mothers feed their young on their milk.

**alphabet**

a b c d e f g h i j k l

**Mm**

n o p q r s t u v w x y z

**picture to help understanding**

**magnet**
Magnets attract iron and steel. Two magnets can attract or repel each other.

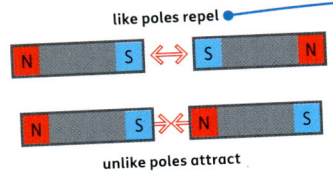

like poles repel

N   S   ⟷   S   N

N   S   ⟩⟨   N   S

unlike poles attract

**manufactured**
Things that are made in factories are manufactured.

**helpful labels**

**mask**
A mask is a cover that you can wear over your face. People wear masks to protect their faces or to change the way they look.

People sometimes wear masks to stop spreading germs through sneezing, coughing and breathing.

**avatars give extra facts and information**

**magnify**
When a small object is magnified, it looks bigger.

57

**page number**

5

B
C
D
E
F
G
H
I
J
K
L
M
N
O
P
Q
R
S
T
U
V
W
X
Y
Z

# Aa
## is for **ant**

## absorb
A material absorbs liquid if it soaks it up.

*The cloth **absorbs** water but the table does not.*

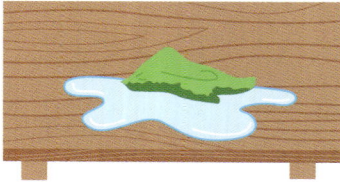

## add
You make numbers bigger when you add.

$$4 + 3 = 7$$

## addition
Addition is adding things together. The sign for addition is $+$.

$$4 + 6 = 10$$

## adult
Adults are fully grown animals and people.

*A dog is an **adult**. A puppy is a young dog.*

adult          puppy

## after
After means coming next.

*13 comes **after** 12.*
*Tuesday comes **after** Monday.*

## age
Your age is the number of years you have lived.

## air
Air is the invisible gas all around us. We breathe air to stay alive.

## algorithm

An algorithm is a set of rules in a computer program. It shows the steps you need to solve a problem.

## alive

Living things are alive. They can feed, grow and reproduce themselves. Animals have senses like seeing, touching and hearing. Plants can sense gravity and their roots always grow downwards.

## along

You can move along a number track forwards or backwards.

1 2 3 4 5 6    **move along forwards**

1 2 3 4 5 6    **move along backwards**

## altogether

'How many altogether?' means add them together.

*There are seven buttons **altogether**.*

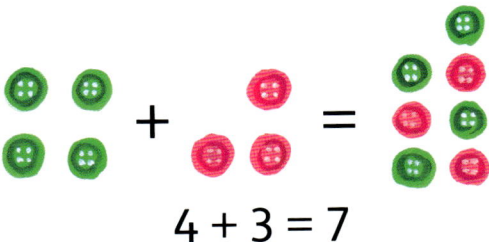

$$4 + 3 = 7$$

## amphibian

Amphibians begin life in the water, as tadpoles. When they grow up they can live on land as well.

*Frogs, toads and newts are all **amphibians**.*

## angle

An angle is the space between two lines or surfaces that meet.

## animal

Animals are living things that eat plants or other animals.

**Did you know that humans are a type of animal?**

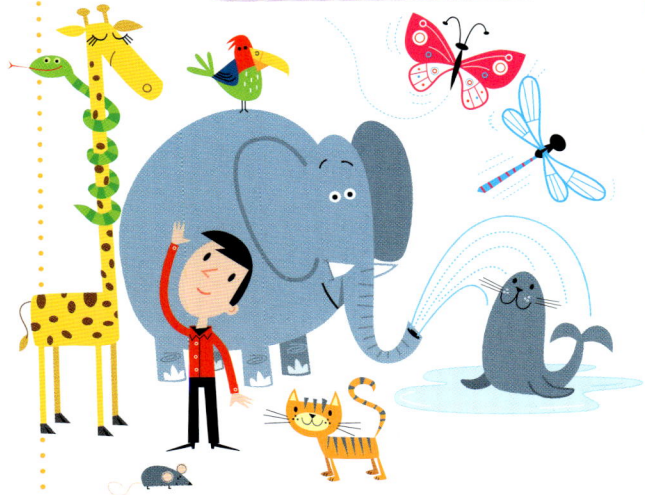

## ankle

Your ankle is where your foot joins your leg. Ankles are joints.

ankle

## answer

You work out a problem to get the answer.

*What is the **answer**?*

7 − 5 = ?

The answer is 2.

## antenna

An antenna is a feeler on the head of some tiny animals. The plural of antenna is antennae.

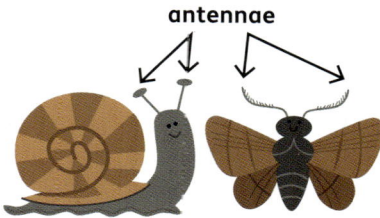

antennae

## antibiotic

Antibiotics are drugs. They cure illnesses caused by bacteria (tiny germs).

antibiotic

## anticlockwise

Anticlockwise is when something turns the opposite way to the hands of a clock.

*The opposite of **anticlockwise** is clockwise.*

clockwise          anticlockwise

## antivirus

Antivirus is software that finds and removes viruses from your computer.

## app

App is short for application or application software. You can download an app to any computer, smartphone or tablet.

I've got a new app for making my photos look better.

## AR

AR stands for augmented reality. It is a way of adding extra information to a real-life scene. This is done by wearing special glasses or using the video display of your smartphone.

## arm

Animals that walk on two legs have arms at the top of their body.

## asthma

Asthma is an illness that makes it difficult to breathe.

*An inhaler helps someone with **asthma** to breathe.*

## attract

If one object is pulled towards another, we say it is attracted.

*A magnet **attracts** iron and steel objects.*

## autumn

Autumn is the time of the year when leaves fall off the trees and it gets colder.

Evergreens do not lose their leaves in autumn. Look up the word *evergreen* on page 34.

## avatar

An avatar is the character you choose to play in a computer game. You can choose a name that is not your name or choose a picture that does not look like you.

## axis

Each red line on this graph is an axis. You say axes when you talk about more than one axis.

*This graph has two **axes**.*

Aa

f
g
h
i
j
k
l
m
n
o
p
q
r
s
t
u
v
w
x
y
z

# B b

is for **bat**

## baby

A baby is a young animal.

A **baby** hen is a chick and a **baby** horse is a foal.

## back

Your back is the part of your body that is behind you, between your neck and your bottom. Your backbone runs down the middle of your back.

**Backs** bend both ways.

## backup

A backup is a copy of a file that you make and keep somewhere safe in a computer.

*If you lose the main file, you can get it back again by using the **backup**.*

## backwards

When you count backwards, the numbers get smaller.

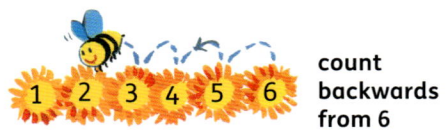

count backwards from 6

**Can you try counting backwards from 10?**

## bacteria

Bacteria are tiny living things that can make us ill. The singular of bacteria is bacterium.

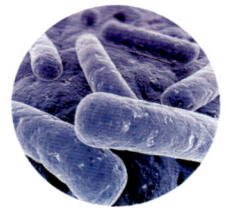

## bake

When you bake food, you heat it in an oven.

*Food changes when it is **baked**.*

## balance

Two sides balance when they are as heavy as each other.

balances

does not balance

## battery

Batteries store electricity.

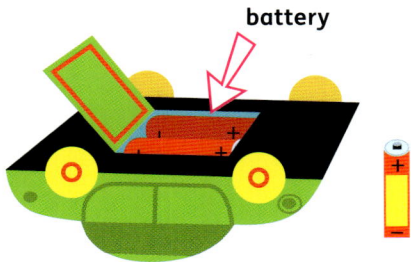

battery

## beak

A bird's beak is its mouth.

*The shape of a bird's **beak** depends on what it eats.*

## bee

A bee is an insect with wings. Some types of bees make honey and live in a beehive.

Some types of bees live on their own in small holes in the ground, trees or walls.

## before

Before means coming in front of.

3 4 5 6 7 8

*6 comes **before** 7.*

January
February
March

*January comes **before** February.*

## bend

A bend is a part of a road or river that curves round.

bend

## berry

Berries are small, round, juicy fruits.

## big

You use big when describing the size of things.

big        bigger        biggest

## bird

Birds are animals with feathers, wings and a beak.

*Ostriches are the world's largest **birds** and hummingbirds are the smallest.*

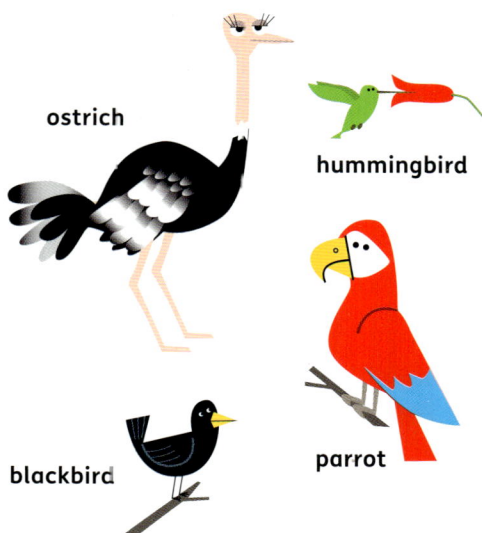

ostrich

hummingbird

parrot

blackbird

## birth

At birth a baby comes out of its mother's body. Mammals give birth to babies. Most other animals hatch from eggs.

*A whale mother gives **birth** under water. She pushes the baby to the surface to breathe.*

## blind

Blind people and animals cannot see.

*The guide dog sees for its owner, who is **blind**.*

## block graph

A block graph is made up of blocks.

*This **block graph** tells you how many children like each colour.*

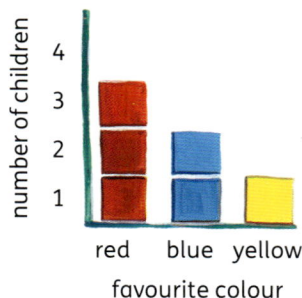

number of children

4
3
2
1

red    blue   yellow

favourite colour

## blood

Blood is a red liquid that takes food and oxygen to all parts of the body.

*When you cut yourself, **blood** leaks out. But it soon goes hard and forms a scab.*

blood

scab

## blossom

Blossom is the flowers on a tree.

## body

The body is all the parts of an animal.

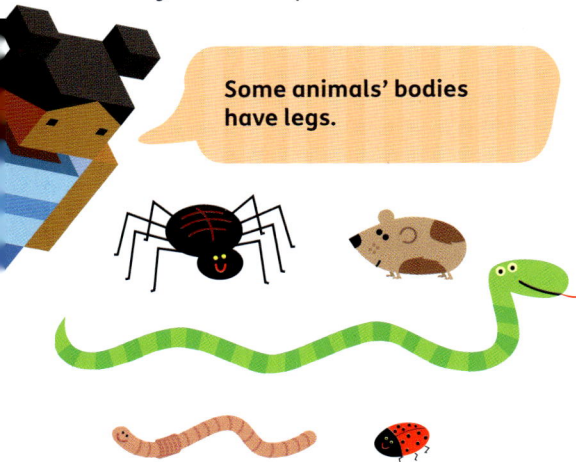

Some animals' bodies have legs.

## boil

Liquids bubble when they boil.

*You have to heat a liquid to make it **boil**.*

## bones

Bones make the hard frame of our body. Most skeletons are made of bone.

***Bones** show up on X-rays.*

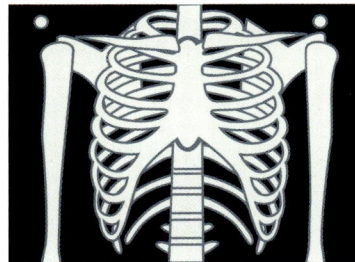

## brain

Brains control thinking and movement.

Patch, dinner!

## branch

A branch grows out from the trunk of a tree.

## brick

A brick is a block made from baked clay. People use bricks for building houses.

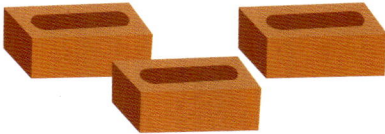

## browse

When you browse on a computer, you look at different websites using a browser.

*She is **browsing** on the internet.*

## browser

A browser is software that allows you to look at websites.

If I want to look at a website, I open a browser. There are lots of different browsers to choose from.

## bubble

Bubbles are little pockets of gas in a liquid.

*The outside of a soap **bubble** is a thin layer of liquid.*

## bud

Buds are flowers or leaves that have not opened yet.

*The leaf or flower is tightly folded inside the **bud**.*

## bug

❶ A bug is an insect.

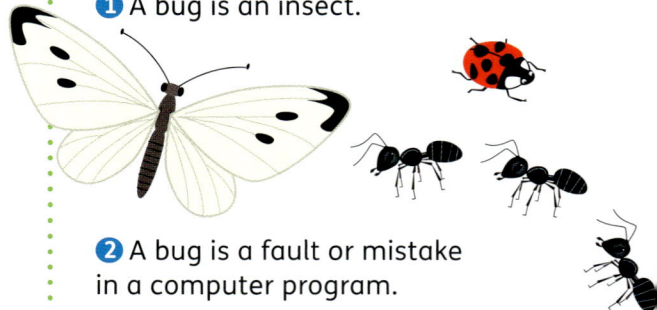

❷ A bug is a fault or mistake in a computer program.

## bulb

Light bulbs glow when electricity passes through them.

## burn

When an object burns, it gives off heat. Flames rise from burning things.

## bush

A bush is a woody plant. It does not have a tall trunk like a tree.

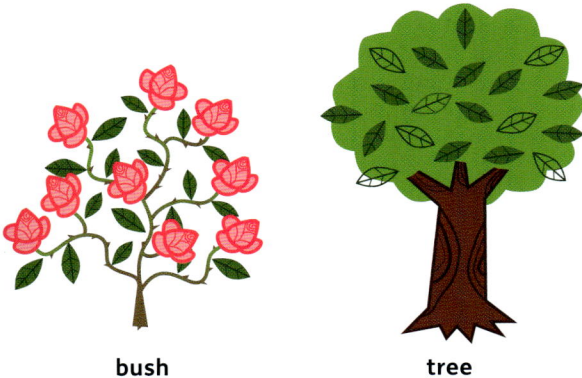

bush

tree

## butterfly

A butterfly is an insect with large, colourful wings.

## button

You press the buttons on a device like a calculator or a mouse.

## buy

When you buy something, you pay money for it.

*Archie **buys** a new ball and puts it in the bag.*

## buzzer

A buzzer makes a sound when it is in a complete electric circuit.

Look up the word *circuit* on page 19.

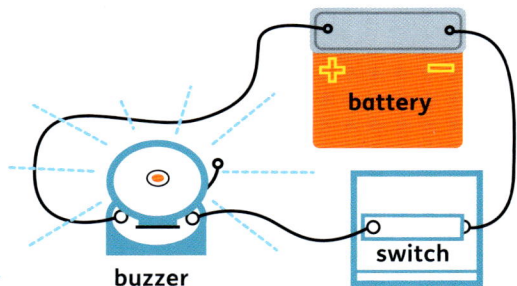

battery

switch

buzzer

# Cc is for crocodile

## cactus

A cactus is a plant that lives in hot, dry places. The plural of cactus is cacti. They have swollen green stems and spines instead of leaves.

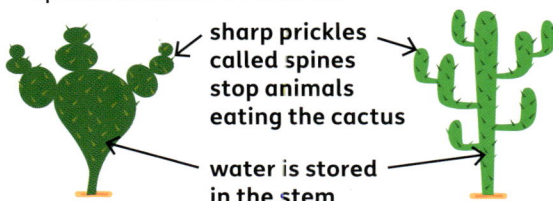

sharp prickles called spines stop animals eating the cactus

water is stored in the stem

## calculate

When you calculate, you work out the answer.

6 + 3 = ?

Answer: 6 + 3 = 9

## calculator

A calculator is a machine that you use to do sums.

35

## calendar

A calendar shows the days, weeks and months in a year.

March

| M | T | W | T | F | S | S |
|---|---|---|---|---|---|---|
| | | 1 | 2 | 3 | 4 | 5 | 6 |
| 7 | 8 | 9 | 10 | 11 | 12 | 13 |
| 14 | 15 | 16 | 17 | 18 | 19 | 20 |
| 21 | 22 | 23 | 24 | 25 | 26 | 27 |
| 28 | 29 | 30 | 31 | | | |

## camera

A camera is for taking pictures. It has a lens to let in light. The light makes a picture on the film. Digital cameras record pictures as digital files.

Smartphones also have cameras.

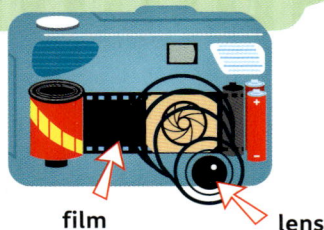

film    lens

## camouflaged

A camouflaged animal is one that blends in with its background.

Spot the **camouflaged** animal.

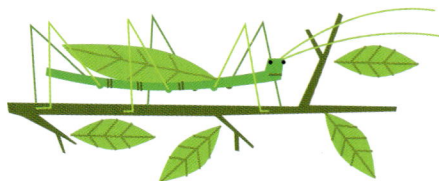

## capacity

Capacity is how much something holds.

This bucket has a **capacity** of 8 litres.

Another word for capacity is volume. Look up the word *volume* on page 100.

## carnivore

Carnivores are animals that eat other animals.

*What do these **carnivores** eat?*

## Carroll diagram

You use a Carroll diagram to sort things into groups.

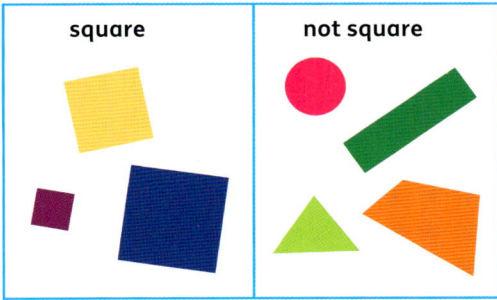

| square | not square |
| --- | --- |

## caterpillar

Caterpillars are a type of larva. They are a stage in the life cycle of many insects.

**Caterpillars** *have long, thin bodies with legs.*

Look up the word *larva* on page 53.

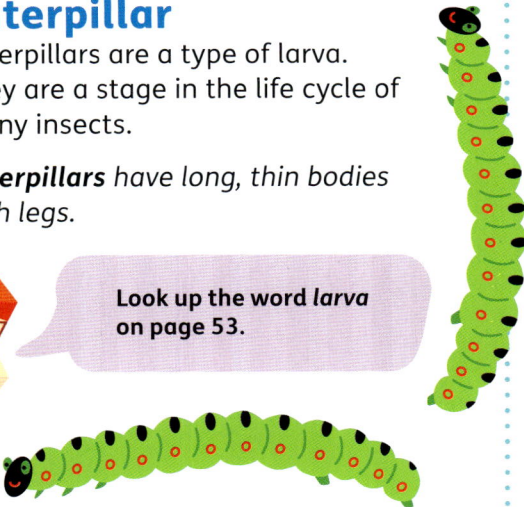

## centimetre

A centimetre is a distance you find on some rulers. 100 centimetres is the same distance as 1 metre.

## centre

The centre of a shape is exactly in the middle.

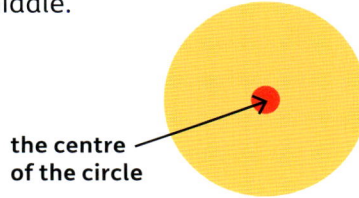

the centre of the circle

## cereal

Cereals are food plants such as wheat, rice, oats and maize. Breakfast cereals are made from these plants.

## change

You get change when you pay too much money for something.

the price    you pay    your change

## chart

A chart shows information using pictures or rows of numbers.

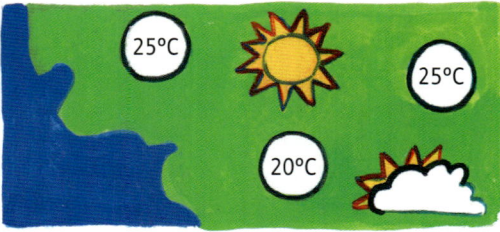

a weather chart

## cheap

Something is cheap when it does not cost a lot of money.

*The teddy is **cheaper** than the tractor.*

cheap        cheaper        cheapest

## chemical

Chemicals are substances that are made in laboratories and factories. Plastics and medicines are chemicals.

**Look up the word *laboratory* on page 53.**

## chick

A chick is a baby bird.

## chicken

A chicken is a bird that is kept on farms for its meat and eggs.

**Did you know that there are more chickens in the world than people?**

## child

A child is a young person.

## circle

A circle is a 2D shape that is perfectly round.

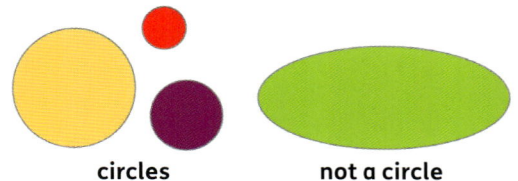

circles        not a circle

# circuit

Electricity travels round an electrical circuit if there is no break in the wires.

If you press the switch, you break the circuit and the light goes out.

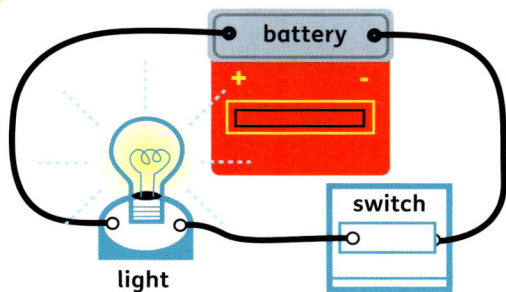

battery

+ -

light

switch

# circular

A circular shape has a circle in it.

*These shapes have **circular** tops.*

# claw

A claw is a sharp part on the end of an arm or leg.

*Many animals have **claws** on their feet. A crab's pincers are **claws**.*

# clay

Clay is dug out of the ground. It can be baked hard to make bricks, tiles and cups.

# click

When you click on something on a computer screen, you go to it and press the mouse button. When you click on something on a touchscreen, you tap it with your finger.

# climate

The climate of a place is the usual weather it has over many years.

# clock

A clock shows you the time.

*Some **clocks** have hands and numbers. Digital **clocks** have only numbers.*

7:00

## clockwise

Clockwise is when something turns the same way as the hands of a clock.

*The opposite of **clockwise** is anticlockwise.*

clockwise          anticlockwise

## close

If you close a computer file, you stop using it.

## cloud

❶ Clouds are made when tiny drops of water form in the air.

A cloud can be two different things. Remember to look at the right meaning!

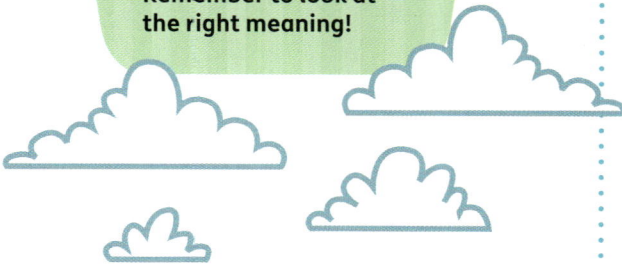

❷ If a computer file is saved on the cloud, it is stored on another computer through the internet.

## coal

Coal is black rock that burns easily. It is made of trees that died millions of years ago.

Burning coal is not good for the environment because it causes pollution.

## cocoon

A cocoon is a silk case that a caterpillar spins around itself when it becomes a pupa.

*Silk comes from silkworm **cocoons**. Silk is used to make clothes.*

Look up the word *pupa* on page 75.

## code

Code is the name for the instructions in a computer program.

## coding

Coding is the name for writing the instructions that make up a computer program. It is also called programming.

## coin

A coin is a piece of money made from metal.

## cold

❶ When something is cold, it is at a low temperature. It is the opposite of hot.

*The drink is **cold**. The ice cream is **colder**. The ice is **coldest**.*

cold    colder    coldest

❷ A cold is an illness that makes you sneeze and your nose run.

## cold-blooded

A cold-blooded animal has about the same temperature as the air or water around it.

*Cold-blooded animals, like reptiles, sunbathe to warm up their bodies.*

## colour

There are millions of colours. We can see colours, but some animals only see in black and white.

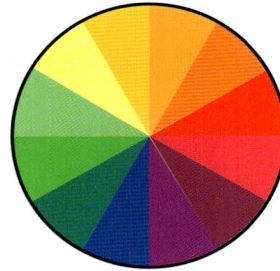

## column

A column of numbers goes up and down.

| 1 | 2 | 3 | 4 |
|---|---|---|---|
| 5 | 6 | 7 | 8 |
| 9 | 10 | 11 | 12 |
| 13 | 14 | 15 | 16 |
| 17 | 18 | 19 | 20 |

a column

## command

A command is a part of a computer program. It tells the computer to do one action, called an operation.

Look up the word *operation* on page 69.

a
b
**Cc**
d
e
f
g
h
i
j
k
l
m
n
o
p
q
r
s
t
u
v

## compost

Compost is a mixture of decayed plants. Tiny animals, fungus and worms help to break down the compost to make soil that is used for growing plants.

*We have a **compost** heap in our garden.*

**Look up the word *fungus* on page 41.**

## computer

A computer is a machine that stores information. Computers can also work things out, or help other machines to work.

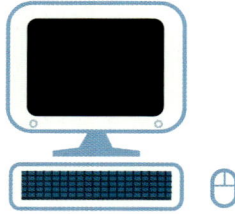

*I sometimes do my homework on the **computer**.*

## conduct

Materials that let electricity pass through them are called conductors.

*The wires in the circuit **conduct** electricity.*

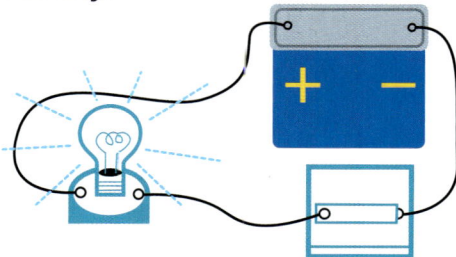

## cone

A cone has one circular end and one pointed end.

## console

You can use a games console to play computer games.

**A computer game can also be called a video game.**

## control

If you control something, you make it do what you want it to do.

*You press these buttons to **control** the robot.*

## cool

To cool something you lower its temperature. Liquids turn into solids when they are cooled.

*When liquid jelly **cools**, it becomes solid.*

## copy

If you copy a file on a computer, you make another file exactly like it. You must give the second file a different name.

## corner

The sides of a shape meet at a corner.

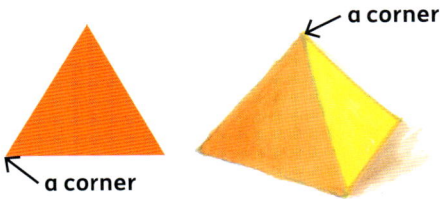

a corner

a corner

## correct

When something is correct, it is right and not wrong.

Which sum is correct?

$4 + 4 = 8$

$4 + 4 = 9$

$4 + 4 = 8$ is the correct sum.

## count

❶ When you count, you say numbers in order.

*I'll **count** up to 10, and you hide.*

❷ To count also means to use numbers to find out how many people or things there are.

*The farmer is **counting** his sheep.*

How many sheep can you count here?

There are six sheep.

## counter

You can use counters to help you add. They can also be used in games and puzzles.

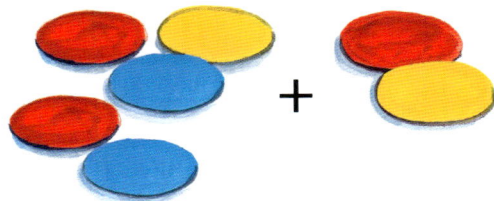

+

$5 + 2 = 7$

## create

To create is to make something new. If you create a computer file, you make a new, empty file for you to use.

## crystal

Crystals are rocks such as salt and diamond. They have regular shapes. Salt crystals are cube-shaped.

*You can grow some **crystals** in a jar.*

## cube

A cube has six square faces.

*All these are **cubes**.*

## cuboid

A cuboid has six rectangular faces, or four rectangular faces and two square faces.

*All these are **cuboids**.*

Choc Crunch

## cursor

On a computer screen, the cursor is a little line or arrow that flashes on and off. It shows where your words will go. You can move the cursor around the screen to go to different places and click on them.

## curve

A curve bends smoothly.

*Here are some **curves**.*

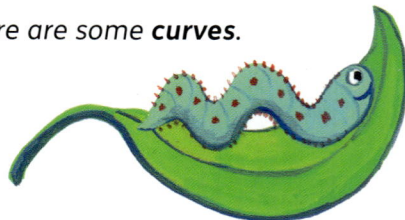

## cut

On a computer, cut and paste are commands that let you move text or pictures from one place to another.

## cyberbully

A cyberbully is someone who bullies over the internet.

**You must tell an adult if someone is mean to you on the internet.**

## cylinder

A cylinder is a 3D shape. It has two flat circular faces and one curved surface.

*All these are **cylinders**.*

# Dd
## is for **dog**

## dark
A place where there is no light is dark.

## data
Data means information you get from facts and numbers.

I asked my friends what their favourite colour was. I recorded the data and made a graph.

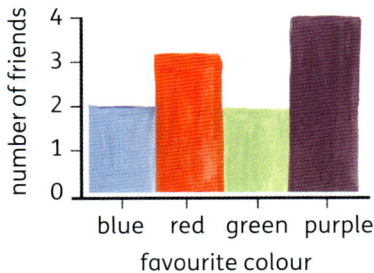

number of friends

4
3
2
1
0

blue  red  green  purple

favourite colour

## database
A database is the collection of all the data you need to do something.

## date
The date tells you the day, the month and the year.

*Leo's **date** of birth is 25th May 2020.*

25th May 2020

## day
During the day, the Sun gives us light. A day can also mean 24 hours.

## dead
A living thing is dead when it stops growing, moving and feeding.

## deaf

A deaf person or animal cannot hear sound.

*Some **deaf** people use sign language.*

Did you know there are lots of different sign languages used around the world?

## dear

When something is dear, it costs a lot of money.

*The blue car is **dearer** than the yellow car.*

dear          dearer          dearest

## debug

To debug a computer program means to find and fix all the things that do not work properly.

## decay

When something decays, it goes rotten and begins to fall apart.

## deciduous

A deciduous tree is a tree that loses its leaves in autumn.

## deep

Deep is how far down or back something goes.

deep

*The fish is swimming in the **deepest** end of the pond.*

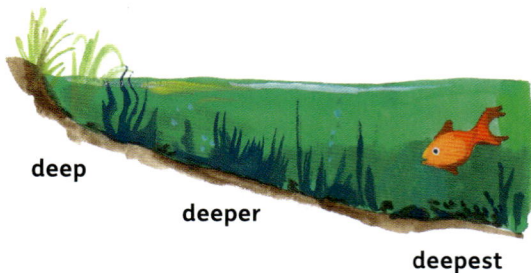

deep

deeper

deepest

## delete

If you delete something, you remove it completely. You can delete a word from something you are writing or typing. You can delete a computer file.

*I **deleted** the title of my story by mistake.*

## depth

Depth is the distance from top to bottom or from front to back.

depth of water

depth of tank

## desktop

The desktop of a computer is what you see on the screen before you open any other windows. It shows all the different programs you can use.

## device

A device is any small piece of equipment.

## diagram

A diagram shows you information in a simple way.

*Here are two kinds of diagram.*

triangles

## diamond

❶ Diamond is a type of crystal. It can be dug from deep in the ground.

*Diamond is the hardest material there is.*

❷ A diamond is a 2D shape with four sides and no right angles. All four sides are the same length.

## diet

An animal's diet is what it eats. A balanced diet for a person contains many types of food.

Cereal

## difference

To find the difference between two numbers you subtract the smaller number from the bigger one.

What is the difference between 7 and 4?

The difference is 3.

## different

When something is different it is not exactly the same.

**different colour**        **different size**

## dig

To dig means to move soil away to make a hole in the ground.

## digest

Animals digest food in their stomach and gut. The food gives them energy and helps them grow.

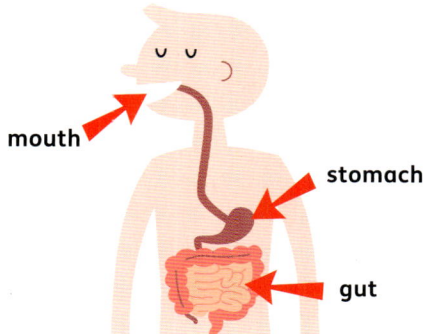

mouth

stomach

gut

## digit

There are ten digits.
They are:

0 1 2 3 4 5 6 7 8 9

The number 14 has two **digits**: 1 and 4. It is a two-**digit** number. **14**

## digital

Digital means 'made of digits'. All the data inside a computer is digital, which means that it is made of 1s and 0s.

## digital clock

A digital clock has no hands.

**a digital clock**     **a digital watch**

## dilute

To dilute something you add more water.

*Juice that has been **diluted** with water does not taste as strong.*

# dinosaur

Dinosaurs were a group of reptiles that died out millions of years ago.

> Scientists learn about dinosaurs by studying fossils.

triceratops

tyrannosaurus

# disease

A disease is an illness. Chickenpox, colds and flu are all diseases.

# dissolve

When a solid dissolves in a liquid it makes a solution. You can see through some solutions.

flour

salt

flour does not dissolve in water

salt dissolves in water

# distance

Distance is how far apart two things are.

distance

# divide

When you divide, you share things out.

*You can **divide** 6 into two equal sets of 3.*

# division

Division is sharing things out. The sign for division is ÷.

$$6 \div 2 = 3$$

a division

# doctor

A doctor is someone whose job is to help people who are sick or hurt to get better.

## document

On a computer, a document is a file that stores information as text and images.

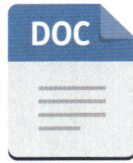

## double

❶ When you double a number, you multiply it by 2.

*Double 5 is 10.*

$$5 \times 2 = 10$$

❷ When you double an object, you fold it in half.

## double-click

Double-click means click a computer mouse button twice, quickly.

## download

To download a file, such as music or a video, means to get a copy of it onto your computer through the internet.

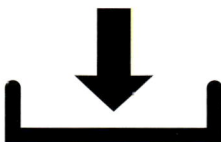

## drag

To drag a computer mouse means to move the mouse while holding the button down. As you drag the mouse, the thing you have clicked on moves with it.

## drug

A drug is a chemical that affects your body. Aspirin is a drug that is used to stop pain. Alcohol is a drug in wine and beer.

## dust

Dust is small specks that float in the air. When they fall, they make objects dusty.

*In countries where there is little rain, there are sometimes **dust** storms.*

## DVD

DVD stands for digital video disk or digital versatile disk. It is a way to store digital data.

# Ee

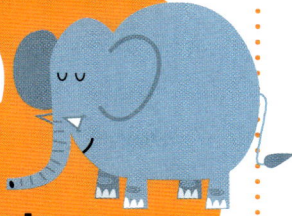

is for **elephant**

## ear

You hear sounds with your ears.

*Ears come in all shapes and sizes.*

## Earth

❶ The planet we live on is called Earth.

*The **Earth** is a huge ball of rock.*

❷ Another name for soil is earth.

## earthquake

When there is an earthquake, the ground suddenly shakes. Strong earthquakes can destroy buildings.

Did you know that when the ground shakes on the Moon, it is called a moonquake?

## echo

An echo is a sound that has bounced back from a wall.

hello

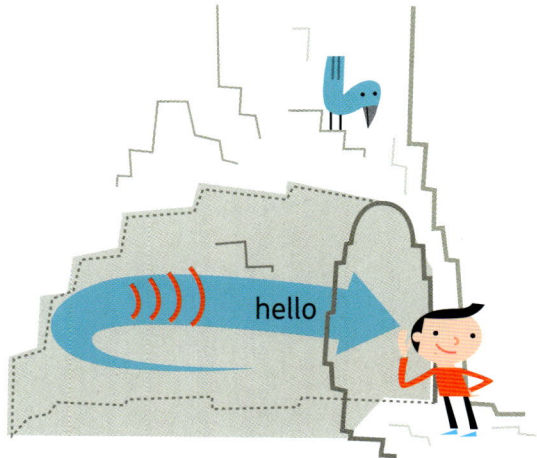
hello

## edge

The edge of a shape is where two faces meet.

curved edge

straight edge

## edit

To edit means to make changes to text or data.

*You can **edit** the file on your computer.*

## egg

Eggs are the starting point for a new animal. Birds lay eggs with hard shells. Crocodiles lay eggs with leathery shells. Frogs lay masses of eggs in jelly.

## elastic

Elastic materials spring back into their original shape.

## elbow

Your elbow is the joint between your upper arm and your lower arm.

*Elbows* work like hinges on a door —they don't twist.

elbow

## electricity

Electricity is a flow of energy. It usually comes from a battery or from the mains.

*All these things work by* **electricity**.

## elephant

An elephant is a very large, grey animal with a very long nose, called a trunk, and big ears.

## email

An email is a message that you send from your computer to someone else's computer.

**I emailed my friend yesterday.**

## emoji

An emoji is a little picture that you can put into an internet message or text message. You add it to show your feelings or for fun.

*She added three laughing* **emojis** *at the end.*

## empty

Something is empty when there is nothing inside it.

empty

## energy

Energy is the ability to do work. This could be lifting, carrying or heating something.

## engine

Engines are machines that can move things. Engines need fuel such as petrol, diesel or coal to work.

a jet engine

*Aeroplanes have jet **engines** on their wings.*

## environment

The environment is the world we live in, especially the plants, animals and things around us.

*Planting more trees will improve our **environment**.*

## equal

When two things are equal, they are worth the same. The sign = tells you two things are the same.

*3 + 3 is **equal** to 6.*

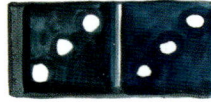

$$3 + 3 = 6$$

## equipment

Equipment is all the things you need for doing something.

*Our school has lots of science **equipment**.*

Go to page 112 to see more science equipment.

microscope

stopwatch

magnifying glass

kitchen scales

torch

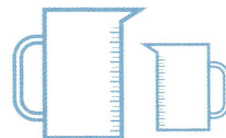

measuring jugs

Ee

a b c d Ee f g h i j k l m q r s t u v w x y z

## equivalent

Equivalent things are worth the same, but they look different.

*Two 5p coins are **equivalent** to one 10p coin.*

5p   5p   10p

## e-safety

E-safety is knowing how to use the computer and the internet safely.

## estimate

When you estimate, you make a sensible guess, not a silly one.

**Estimate the number of marbles in this bag.**

A good estimate is any number between 15 and 21.

## estimation

An estimation is a good guess.

*'The ribbon is about 7 centimetres long' is a good **estimation**.*

## evaporate

When a liquid evaporates, it changes into a gas. Evaporation happens more quickly if the air is warm.

*We want water to **evaporate** from wet washing.*

## even

You can divide all even numbers into twos.

*2  4  6  8  10 are **even** numbers.*

## evergreen

An evergreen is a tree that keeps its green leaves all year.

# exactly

Exactly means neither more nor less.

exactly the same length

nearly the same length

# exchange

When you exchange something, you change it for something else.

# exercise

People and other animals need exercise to keep fit and healthy.

# experiment

When you do an experiment, you try something out and see what happens.

*How do you think this **experiment** will end?*

# explore

When you explore, you look carefully round a place for the first time.

*We went off to **explore** the woods.*

# extinct

When a type of animal or plant is extinct, none are left alive.

*The dodo is an **extinct** bird.*

The dodo went extinct over 300 years ago.

# eye

You see things with your eyes.

*Some animals have large **eyes** to help them see at night.*

# Ff

## is for **frog**

## fabric

Fabric is another name for cloth.

## face

❶ Your face is the front part of your head.

*The **faces** of humans, chimps, gorillas and monkeys have things in common.*

❷ A face is one side of a 3D shape.

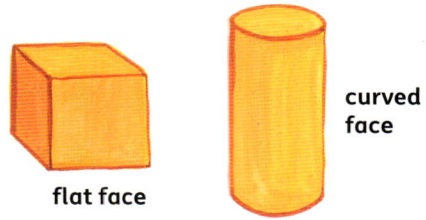

**flat face**

**curved face**

## fast

Fast describes how quickly something moves.

**fast**      **faster**      **fastest**

## fat

Many foods contain fat. Cheese and butter have lots of fat. Vegetables and fruit have only a little fat.

*These are all high-**fat** foods.*

## feather

Birds have feathers. No other animals have them.

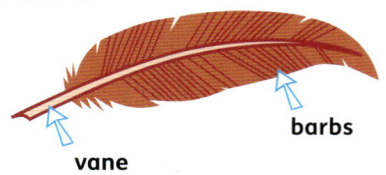

**vane**

**barbs**

## feed

Animals feed on plants or other animals.

## female

Female animals give birth to babies or lay eggs.

Did you know that male seahorses give birth?

## few

Few means a small number of things.

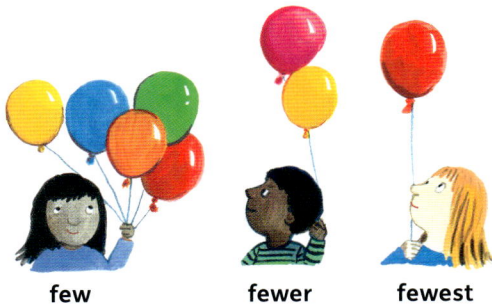

few          fewer          fewest

## figure

When you write the number seventeen in figures, it looks like this: 17.

*These numbers are written in **figures**.*

7

14

76

125

## file

A file is a set of data or programs that is stored in a computer. All files have names so you can find them easily.

DOC     PDF     XLS     PPT

## fin

A fish flaps its fins to help it swim.

dorsal fin

tail fin

pectoral fin

## finger

You have four fingers and a thumb on each hand. They are good for gripping.

*The nails at the end protect the tips of your **fingers**.*

## fire

To start a fire, you need fuel, air and heat.

*Putting water onto a **fire** will put it out.*

a b c d e **Ff** g h i j k l m n o p q r s t u v w x y z

**Ff**

## fish

A fish is an animal that lives in water and breathes through gills.

*There are many different types of **fish**.*

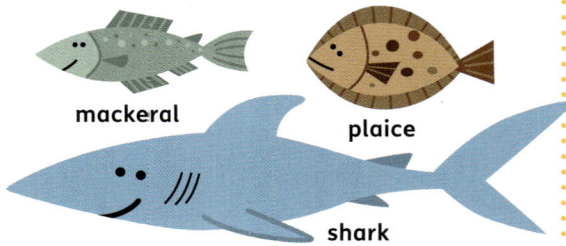

mackeral

plaice

shark

## flame

Flames are produced when a fire is burning.

## flat shape

A flat shape has length and width but no thickness. It is also called a two-dimensional, or 2D, shape.

## flipper

The flippers on animals such as seals or penguins are the flat arms that they use for swimming.

flipper

## float

Objects float in water when they are not resting on the bottom.

*The ball and the fish are both **floating**.*

## flock

A flock is a group of birds or sheep.

## flood

If there is a flood, a lot of water spreads over the land.

## flower

Flowers are the parts of a plant that make seeds.

## fly

Animals that fly can move through the air for long distances.

*Bats, most birds and many insects can all **fly**.*

## fog

Fog is cloud at ground level. You cannot see far in the fog.

***Fog** is made of tiny water droplets.*

## foil

Foil is very thin sheets of metal, used to wrap food.

## folder

A folder is a set of files that are grouped together in a computer.

## food

Animals need food for energy and to help them grow. Plants make their food from water, air and sunlight. You need different types of food to stay healthy, including fruit and vegetables.

## food chain

A food chain is a set of plants and animals that are linked because each one eats the one below it on the chain. For example, seeds are eaten by a mouse, then a mouse is eaten by a bird of prey.

**bird of prey**

**mouse**

**seeds**

## foot

Some animals, including humans, have feet at the end of their legs. Others have hooves, paws or webbed feet at the end of their legs.

## force

Forces can be pushes or pulls.

## fortnight

A fortnight is 2 weeks.

### April

| M | T | W | T | F | S | S |
|---|---|---|---|---|---|---|
| | | | | 1 | 2 | 3 |
| 4 | 5 | 6 | 7 | 8 | 9 | 10 |
| 11 | 12 | 13 | 14 | 15 | 16 | 17 |
| 18 | 19 | 20 | 21 | 22 | 23 | 24 |
| 25 | 26 | 27 | 28 | 29 | 30 | |

## forwards

When you count forwards, the numbers get bigger.

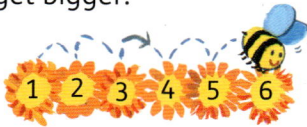

1 2 3 4 5 6

count forwards from 1

## fossil

A fossil is the remains of an animal or plant buried in rocks.

This is a **fossil** of a fern.

## fraction

A fraction is a part of a whole shape or a whole number.

One half or $\frac{1}{2}$ is a fraction.

a fraction of a cake

## freeze

When a liquid freezes, it becomes so cold that it turns to a solid.

Orange juice can be **frozen** to make ice lollies.

## friction

Friction is the force that slows down moving objects.

**Friction** from the brakes slows you down and stops you.

brake

brake

# frog

A frog is a small amphibian with smooth, wet skin and long back legs. Frogs live near water and can jump by using their strong back legs.

**Look up the word *amphibian* on page 7.**

# frost

Frost is ice that looks like white powder and covers the ground when the weather is very cold.

# fruit

Fruit is the fleshy part of a plant that covers a seed.

*Some **fruit** has small seeds, other **fruit** has large stones.*

**Oranges, grapes, apples and tomatoes are all fruit.**

# fuel

A fire needs fuel to help it burn. Engines need fuel to make them work.

fire

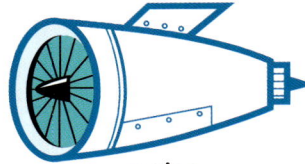

engine

# full

When something is full, there is no space left inside it.

full          half full          empty

# fungus

Mushrooms and toadstools are types of fungus. The plural of fungus is fungi. They feed on decaying plants or animals.

**Look up the word *mushroom* on page 63.**

# Gg

### is for **goat**

## game

You can play games on a computer. There are many types of computer game. Some games have puzzles and some are adventures that you can take part in. A computer game is also called a video game.

## gas

A gas is able to spread out to fill any container.

*A Bunsen burner burns **gas**.*

Air is an invisible gas that is all around us.

## germ

Germs are tiny living things that can make us ill.

*When you sneeze, **germs** shoot out of your nose and mouth.*

Bacteria and viruses are types of germ.

## germinate

A seed germinates when it begins to grow.

*Seeds only need water and warmth to **germinate**.*

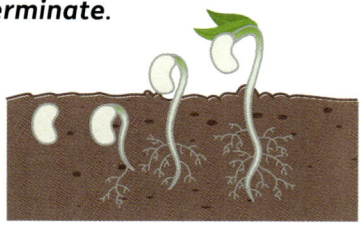

## gill

Fish breathe through their gills.

*Fish take in water through their mouth and push it out through their **gills**.*

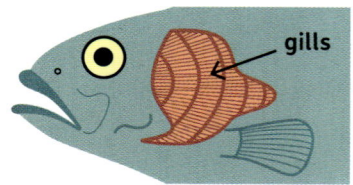

gills

## giraffe

A giraffe is a very tall animal with a long neck and long, thin legs.

## glass

Glass is a hard, shiny, transparent material.

*Glass can be many different colours.*

Look up the word *transparent* on page 96.

## gold

Gold is a shiny, yellow metal that is very valuable.

## gram

You can use grams when you weigh things.

scales weigh in grams

grams

1,000 grams = 1 kilogram

## graph

A graph gives you information.

Here are two different kinds of graph.

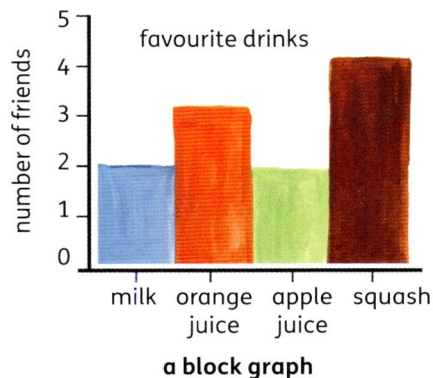

favourite activities

football

cycling

TV

reading

music

**a pictogram**

favourite drinks

number of friends

milk  orange juice  apple juice  squash

**a block graph**

## grass

Grasses are flowering plants that have long, thin leaves.

*Bamboo is a type of giant grass.*

## gravity

The Earth's gravity pulls everything down to the ground.

e
f
**Gg**
h
i
j
k
l
m
n
o
p
q
r
s
t
u
v
w
x
y
z

43

## greater than
Greater than means more than.
The sign for greater than is >.

5 is greater than 2. The > sign tells you which number is the largest.

5 > 2

## grid
The lines on a grid go across each other.

a square grid

a triangular grid

## group
A group is a set of things.

groups of 2

## grow
Living things grow and get larger.

*Trees* **grow** *and get bigger all their lives.*

## growth
Growth is the way in which something grows and gets bigger.

*We measured the* **growth** *of the plants.*

## gut
Your gut is where most of your food is digested.

Tummy is another word for gut.

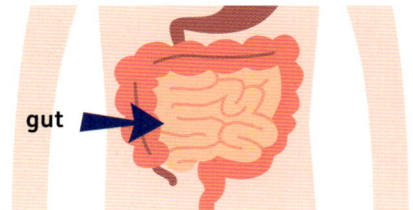

gut

# Hh

is for **hedgehog**

## habitat
Habitat is the place where an animal or plant lives.

Some birds live on the seashore, which is their habitat.

## hair
Hairs are thin threads that grow from the skin of many animals. Some plants have hairs, too.

## half
When you divide something in half, each part is the same size. You can write half as $\frac{1}{2}$.

**half**

**not half**

## half turn
A half turn is when you make half of a whole turn.

**start**

**a half turn**

**a whole turn**

## half way
Half way is in the middle.

half way

a b c d e f g Hh i j k l m n o p q r s t u v w x y z

## halve

When you halve something, you divide it into two equal parts.

*Jack **halves** his pear.*

## hand

Some clocks and watches have hands.

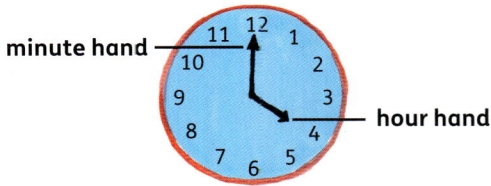

minute hand — 11 12 1 10 2 9 3 8 4 7 6 5 — hour hand

## hard

Something that cannot easily be cut or squashed is hard.

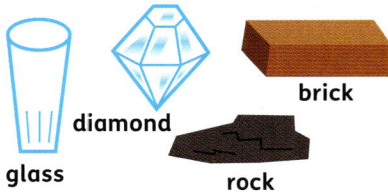

diamond

brick

glass

rock

## head

The head is the part of the body at the top or front.

*Most animals have their brains, eyes, ears and mouth in their **heads**.*

## heal

When a cut or a broken bone heals, it gets better.

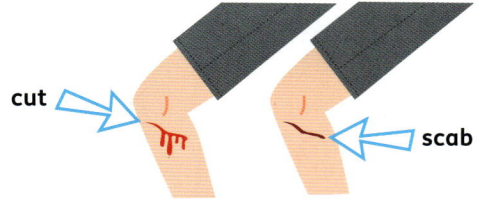

cut

scab

## healthy

A person, animal or plant is healthy if their body is working well.

## heart

An animal's heart pushes blood around its body.

*The **heart** is a muscle in our chest that works all the time we are alive.*

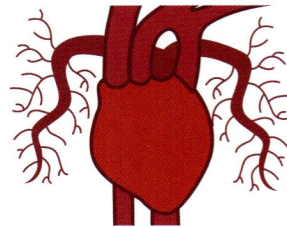

Did you know that an octopus has three hearts?

## heat

Heat is a form of energy. Flames give off heat.

*The Earth is **heated** by the Sun.*

## heavy

You use heavy to describe the weight of something.

**heavy**          **heavier**          **heaviest**

## height

Height is how tall something is or how far it is from the ground.

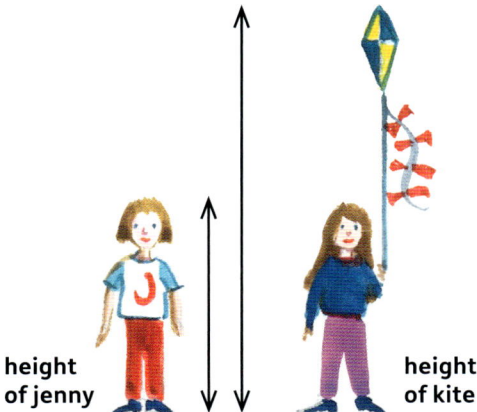

height of jenny          height of kite

## herbivore

A herbivore is an animal that only eats plants.

## herd

A herd is a large group of animals that live and feed together.

## hexagon

A hexagon is a 2D shape with six straight sides.

*All these are **hexagons**.*

## hill

A hill is land that is higher than the land around it. Hills are smaller than mountains.

A B C D E F G **Hh** I J K L M N O P Q R S T U V W X Y Z

## hollow

A hollow shape is empty inside.

a hollow cube    a hollow cylinder

## honey

Honey is a sweet, sticky food made by bees.

## horse

A horse is an animal with hoofs that is used for riding and pulling things.

## hour

One hour is 60 minutes long. There are 24 hours in each day.

*One **hour** has passed.*

## hour hand

The hour hand on a clock is the shortest hand.

**Look at the clock below. What time is it?**

minute hand

hour hand

The answer is 9 o'clock.

## human

You are a human. Humans are a type of animal.

*All people are **human**.*

## hygiene

Hygiene is the state of being clean and free of germs.

**Practise good hygiene by washing your hands regularly.**

soap

# Ii

is for **iguana**

## ice

Ice is the solid form of water.

*Water turns to **ice** when it gets very cold.*

Icicles, snowflakes and a frozen pond are forms of ice.

## icon

An icon is a little picture that stands for an app, file or task. You click on the icon to choose the one you want to use.

## incubate

To incubate something is to keep it warm by adding heat. Birds incubate their eggs by keeping them warm with their bodies. Baby mammals have to be kept warm too.

## infect

If you are infected with germs, they can make you ill.

## input

Input is the data that you put into a computer.

## insect

An insect is an animal with six legs.

*All **insects** have three parts to their body.*

Ants, butterflies and bees are all insects.

## instruction

An instruction is a part of a computer program. It tells the computer to do something.

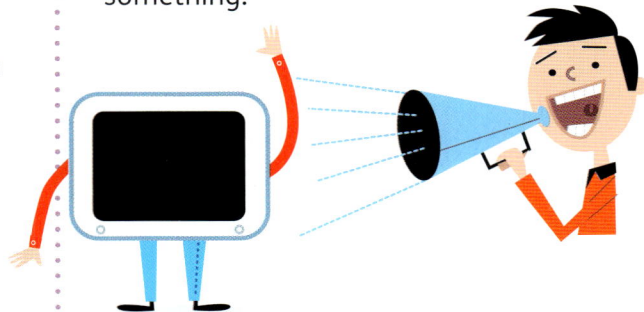

## insulate

If you insulate a hot object, you keep it warm.

*You can use a flask to **insulate** a hot liquid from the cold air.*

## internet

People use the internet so that computers all over the world can get information and send messages to each other.

**The word internet was first used in the 1970s.**

## inverse

The opposite of something is the inverse.

*Multiplication is the **inverse** of division.*

## investigate

When you investigate, you look for an answer.

***Investigate** the missing numbers.*

$$\square + \square = 7$$

## iPad™

An iPad™ is a type of tablet.

## iPhone™

An iPhone™ is a type of smartphone.

## irregular shape

The sides of an irregular shape are not all the same length.

**irrregular shapes**

# Jj

## is for jellyfish

## jaw

The bones around the mouth are the jaw.

*Teeth are fixed into the **jaw** bones.*

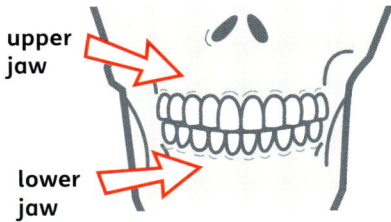

upper jaw

lower jaw

## join

You can join up things with a line.

*The lines **join** each number to a set.*

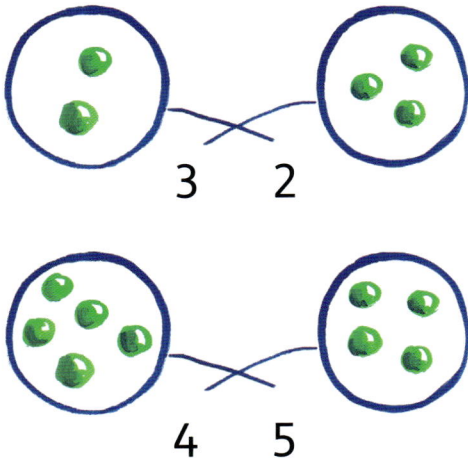

3    2

4    5

## joint

A joint is a place where two bones are joined together.

> Your shoulder, elbow, wrist and fingers are all joints.

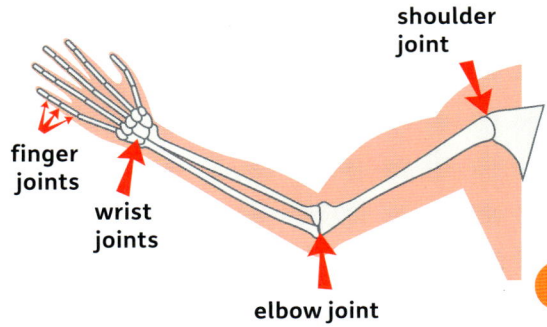

shoulder joint

finger joints

wrist joints

elbow joint

## jungle

A jungle is a thick forest in a warm, wet part of the world.

# Kk

is for **kangaroo**

## keyboard

You use a keyboard to put text, data or commands into a computer.

## kilogram

You use kilograms when you weigh heavy things.

1 kilogram = 1,000 grams

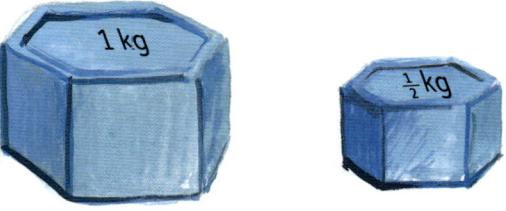

1 kg

$\frac{1}{2}$ kg

## kite

❶ A kite is a light toy that you can fly in the wind at the end of a long piece of string.

❷ A kite is a 2D shape with four straight sides. It has two pairs of sides that are the same length.

## knee

Your knee is the joint between your upper leg and your lower leg.

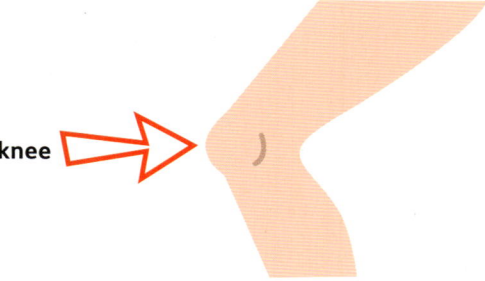

knee

A B C D E F G H I J Kk L M N R S T U V W X Y Z

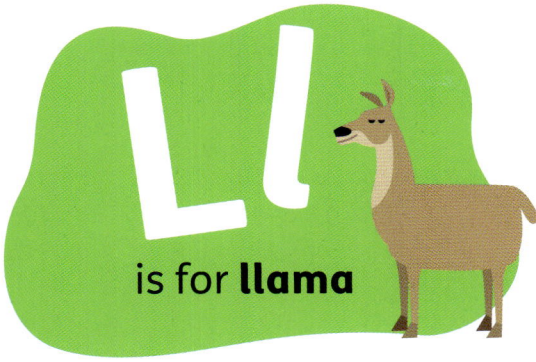

# Ll

is for **llama**

## label

A label tells you what something is.
A title is a label.

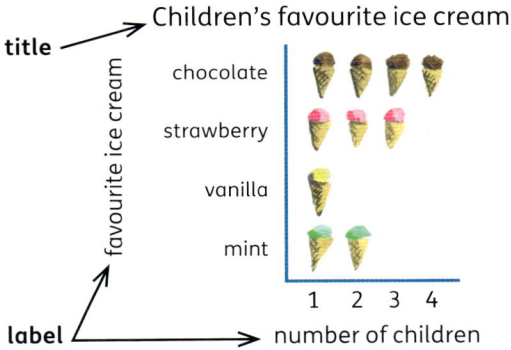

Children's favourite ice cream

title →

favourite ice cream

chocolate

strawberry

vanilla

mint

1  2  3  4

label → number of children

## laboratory

A laboratory is a room in which people do scientific experiments.

## ladybird

A ladybird is a small flying beetle. Most ladybirds are red with black spots.

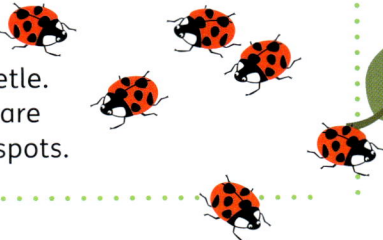

## laptop

A laptop is a computer that has the keyboard and screen built into it.

## large

Large describes the size of something.

large    larger    largest

## larva

A larva is the caterpillar stage in the life cycle of many insects. The plural of larva is larvae. Larvae hatch from eggs.

**Look up *life cycle* on page 54.**

## leaf

Plants make food in their leaves.

*Most **leaves** are green.*

## least

The least amount is the smallest.

Which cup has the least juice?

The answer is the middle one.

## left

One side of your body is the left side.

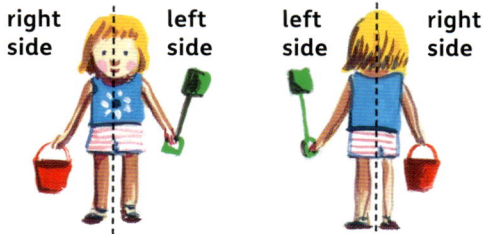

right side · left side · left side · right side

## legs

Your legs are the parts of your body between your hips and your feet.

leg

leg

## length

Length is how long something is.

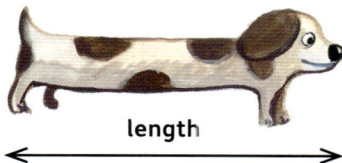

length

## less than

Less than means not as many as.
The sign for less than is <.

3 is less than 5.
The < sign tells you which number is the smallest.

3 < 5

## lice

The small insects that can live in people's hair are head lice.

*Lice* suck blood and make your head itch.

## life cycle

A life cycle is made up of the stages of a living thing's life.

The **life cycle** of a butterfly has four stages.

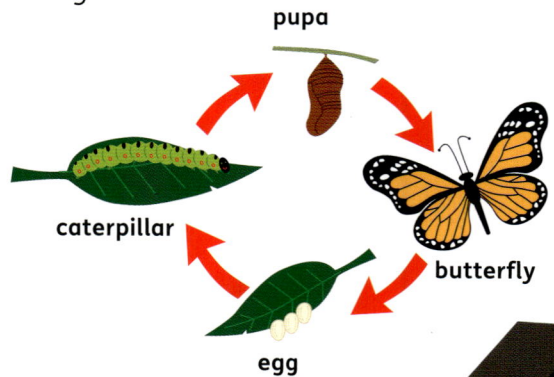

pupa

caterpillar

butterfly

egg

Look up the word *pupa* on page 75.

## light

Light is a form of energy that we can see with our eyes.

*Light comes from many sources.*

## limb

A limb is the arm or leg of an animal.

Some minibeasts have a lot of limbs.

## line

A line can be straight or curved.

a straight line　　a curved line

## line of symmetry

The two sides of a line of symmetry are the same.

*A line of symmetry is like a mirror because one side is a reflection of the other.*

a line of symmetry

## lion

A lion is a large, wild cat. A male lion has long fur around its head.

## liquid

Liquids can flow. The surface of a liquid is level.

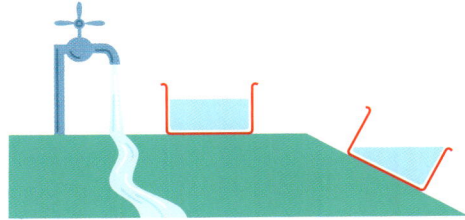

## list

In a list you write things under each other.

milk
apples
bread
cake
cheese

Joe
Fatima
Tom
Wendy
Lea
Ben
James

## litre

You use litres when you measure the volume of something. It is usually used to measure liquids or gases.

1,000 millilitres = 1 litre

1 litre of milk　　half a litre of milk

A B C D E F G H I J K Ll M N O P Q R S T U V W X Y Z

## living
Something that is living is alive.

## lizard
A lizard is an animal with a long body, four legs and a long tail. Lizards are reptiles.

## log
❶ A log is a part of a tree that has been chopped down. You can burn logs on a fire.

❷ When you log in to a computer, you switch it on so that you can use it. When you log out, you shut it down and switch it off.

*You might need your username and password to **log** in.*

Log in
username
password

Log in

**Look up the word *password* on page 72.**

## logic
Logic is an organized way of thinking and working things out.

*You use **logic** to complete a puzzle.*

## long
Long describes the length of something.

*You place things side by side to find the **longest**.*

long
longer
longest

## loud
Something loud is easy to hear.

*Suddenly, there was a **loud** bang.*

## lungs
Many animals breathe air through lungs. Some tiny animals, such as insects, do not have lungs.

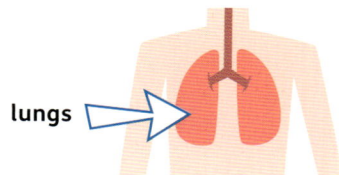

lungs

# Mm
## is for **mole**

## machine
Machines help us do work.

## magnet
Magnets attract iron and steel. Two magnets can attract or repel each other.

**like poles repel**

**unlike poles attract**

## magnify
When a small object is magnified, it looks bigger.

## male
A male animal does not give birth or lay eggs.

*A cockerel is a **male** chicken.*

## mammal
Mammals are furry or hairy animals. Mammal mothers feed their young on their milk.

## manufactured
Things that are made in factories are manufactured.

## mask
A mask is a cover that you can wear over your face. People wear masks to protect their faces or to change the way they look.

People sometimes wear masks to stop spreading germs through sneezing, coughing and breathing.

## mass

When you weigh something, you find out its mass.

*The elephant has a bigger mass than the mouse.*

## material

Material is the stuff that objects are made from.

*Cloth, plastic and wood are all types of material.*

## mature

Mature means fully grown or developed.

## measure

You measure something to find out its size, how much it weighs or how much it holds.

## measurement

A measurement is a number that tells you about the size, weight or volume of something.

110
100
90
80
70
60
50
40
30
20
10
0

**height 104 centimetres**    **weight 21 kilograms**

## medicine

Drugs that make you better are called medicines.

# melt

When solids turn to liquid, they melt.

*Solid ice cream **melts** quickly when it is warm.*

# memory

❶ You use your memory when you remember things.

❷ The memory of a computer is where the computer holds all the data and instructions it is using.

memory card

# menu

A menu is a list of choices. On a computer, you click on the choice you want.

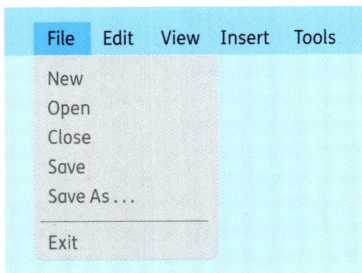

| File | Edit | View | Insert | Tools |
|------|------|------|--------|-------|

New
Open
Close
Save
Save As . . .

Exit

# message

A message or a text message is a short written message you can send from your phone to someone else's phone.

A text message is sometimes called a text.

# metal

Metals are hard, shiny and cold to the touch.

*Some **metal** objects ring when you hit them.*

# metre

You use metres to measure the length of something. A metre can be broken into smaller units called centimetres.

1 metre = 100 centimetres

## metre stick

A metre stick is like a long ruler. It is 100 centimetres long.

a metre stick

## micro-habitat

A micro-habitat is a small place where an animal or plant lives that exists within a larger one.

## microscope

Looking through a microscope makes really tiny objects look bigger.

*Even an insect's legs look big under a microscope.*

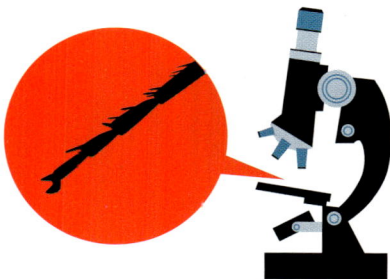

## middle

In the middle means in the centre.

**6 7 8**     *7 is in the middle.*

*The spider is in the middle.*

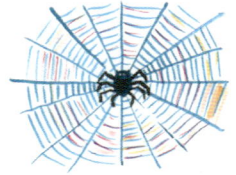

## milk

Young mammals drink milk from their mother's body.

## minibeast

Minibeasts are small animals. They do not have bones inside them.

*Most minibeasts have a hard covering.*

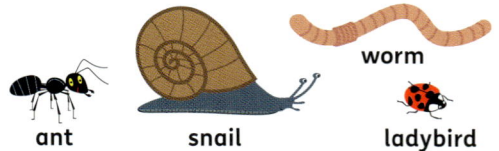

worm

ant          snail          ladybird

## minus

Minus is another name for the subtraction sign, −.

$$7 - 4 = 3$$

## minute

A minute is a short time.
There are 60 minutes in 1 hour.

5 **minutes** have passed.

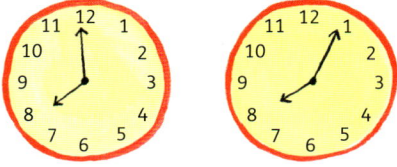

## minute hand

The minute hand moves all the way round the clock in 1 hour.

minute hand

## mirror

A surface that shows a reflection acts as a mirror. Many shiny surfaces show reflections.

## mirror line

A mirror line is like a mirror. One half of the picture is a reflection of the other half.

a mirror line

## mobile phone

A mobile phone is a phone that can send and receive messages without being plugged in.

A mobile phone that you can also use as a computer is called a smartphone.

## monitor

A monitor is the part of a computer that has a screen.

## monkey

A monkey is an animal that lives in the trees. It swings and climbs using its hands, feet and long tail.

## month

A month is part of a year. There are 12 months in a year.

Go to page 116 to see all 12 months of the year.

| March | | | | | | | | April | | | | | | |
|---|---|---|---|---|---|---|---|---|---|---|---|---|---|---|
| M | T | W | T | F | S | S | | M | T | W | T | F | S | S |
| | 1 | 2 | 3 | 4 | 5 | 6 | | | | | | 1 | 2 | 3 |
| 7 | 8 | 9 | 10 | 11 | 12 | 13 | | 4 | 5 | 6 | 7 | 8 | 9 | 10 |
| 14 | 15 | 16 | 17 | 18 | 19 | 20 | | 11 | 12 | 13 | 14 | 15 | 16 | 17 |
| 21 | 22 | 23 | 24 | 25 | 26 | 27 | | 18 | 19 | 20 | 21 | 22 | 23 | 24 |
| 28 | 29 | 30 | 31 | | | | | 25 | 26 | 27 | 28 | 29 | 30 | |

a b c d h i j k l Mm n o p q r v w x y z

## Moon

The Moon is a rocky ball that goes round the Earth. Other planets have moons going round them too.

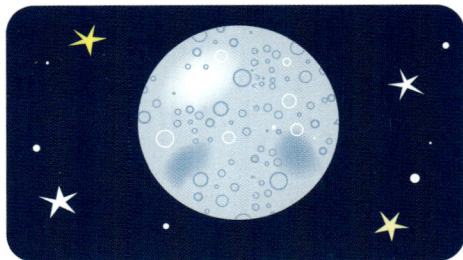

## most

Most means the largest amount.

Fred has the most apples.

Alice        Mina        Fred

## motor

Motors are machines that are used to move objects.

*Many forms of transport use **motors**.*

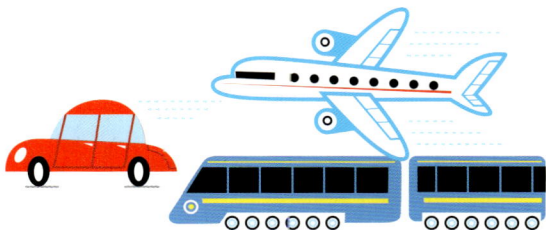

## mould

A tiny fungus which grows on other living things is called mould. Mouldy foods can be bad for us, but blue cheeses are made mouldy on purpose.

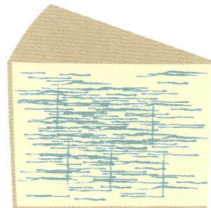

## mountain

A mountain is a very high hill.

## mouse

❶ A mouse is a very small animal with a long tail and a pointed nose.

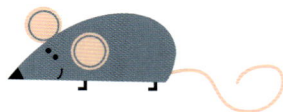

❷ A mouse is also a small box with buttons that you click to move things around on a computer screen.

## mouth

A mouth is an opening on the head that is used for eating and breathing.

*Many animals have teeth in their **mouths** and some have long tongues.*

## multiple

The multiples of a number are the numbers that it will divide into exactly. Here are some multiples of 2, 5 and 10.

The multiples go on and on.

**multiples of 2**
2, 4, 6, 8, 10 . . .

**multiples of 5**
5, 10, 15, 20, 25 . . .

**multiples of 10**
10, 20, 30, 40, 50 . . .

## multiplication

Multiplication is when you multiply numbers together. The multiplication sign is ✕.

$3 \times 2 = 6$

## multiply

When you multiply, you add the same number again and again.

Multiply 3 by 4.
What is the answer?

The answer is 12.

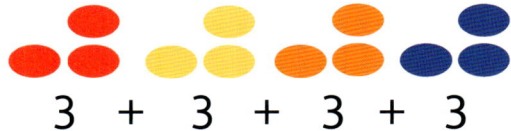

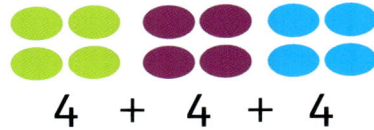

$3 + 3 + 3 + 3$

$4 + 4 + 4$

## muscle

Muscles are parts of your body that pull on your bones so you can move.

*Your legs have big **muscles**.*

## mushroom

A mushroom is a type of fungus that grows in the earth and looks like a little umbrella.

# Nn
is for **newt**

## narrow

When something is narrow, its sides are close together.

wide

narrow

## natural

Something is said to be natural if it happens without human help.

*The plants in a rainforest grow **naturally**.*

All these are natural objects.

## neck

A head and body are joined by a neck.

*Giraffes have longer **necks** than zebras so they can eat food from the treetops.*

## network

A network is a group of computers that can work together.

## new

❶ You use the word new when talking about something that is not old.

new

old

❷ New can mean different from the one before.

*I'm starting at a **new** school tomorrow.*

## night

Night is the time when it is dark because the Sun is shining on the other side of the world.

*At **night**, we can see stars far away in space.*

## none

None is when you have nothing.

four carrots    none

## non-living

Something that has never been alive is non-living.

*Rock, metal and glass are **non-living**.*

## nose

Many animals have a nose on the front of their head. They use it for smelling.

Rescue dogs can smell people buried under the snow.

## nought

Nought is another word for nothing, none or zero.

## number

You can represent numbers in many different ways.

some ways to show the number 4

## number bond

Here are some number bonds.

| addition bond | $3 + 4 = 7$ |
| subtraction bond | $5 - 1 = 4$ |
| multiplication bond | $2 \times 3 = 6$ |
| division bond | $10 \div 2 = 5$ |

## number fact

Here are some number facts for 5. You can use numbers and words.

$$5 = 3 + 2$$

$$5 = 10 \div 2$$

$$5 \text{ is } 3 \text{ more than } 2$$

Can you think of some number facts for other numbers?

## number line

In a number line the numbers are in order. Each number marks a point on the line.

1   2   3   4   5

## number pair

A number pair is two numbers that go together.

5 and 0

**5, 0**

All these **number pairs** equal 5.

3 and 2

**3, 2**

4 and 1

**4, 1**

## number sentence

A number sentence uses words or numbers.

6 take away 2 leaves 4

3 more than 5 makes 8

$4 + 6 = 10$

## number square

In a number square a number is written inside each square.

Put your finger on the number 11 and count on 6 squares.

What is the answer?

The answer is 17.

| 1 | 2 | 3 | 4 | 5 |
|----|----|----|----|----|
| 6 | 7 | 8 | 9 | 10 |
| 11 | 12 | 13 | 14 | 15 |
| 16 | 17 | 18 | 19 | 20 |
| 21 | 22 | 23 | 24 | 25 |

**a 25 number square**

## number track

In a number track the numbers are in order. Each number takes up a space on the line.

| 1 | 2 | 3 | 4 | 5 | 6 | 7 | 8 | 9 | 10 |

## numeral

A numeral shows the symbol of a number. We can also write the number word.

3    three    III

## nut

A nut is a kind of dry fruit that you can eat after you have taken off its hard shell.

Some people cannot eat nuts because it makes them unwell.

## nutrition

Nutrition is the food someone needs to keep them alive and healthy.

Cereal

# Oo

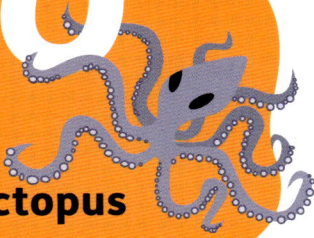

is for **octopus**

## object

An object is anything that you can see, touch or hold.

## oblong

An oblong is a shape that is longer than it is wide.

oblongs

## observation

Observation is the act of watching something carefully.

## ocean

An ocean is a big sea.

*They sailed across the Atlantic **Ocean**.*

## octagon

An octagon is a 2D shape with eight straight sides.

These shapes are all octagons. Go to page 120 for more shapes.

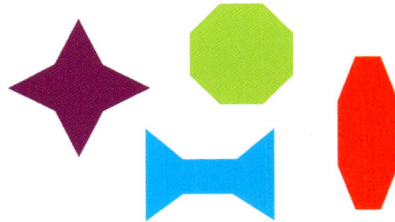

## o'clock

You use o'clock to say what time it is.

*I'll meet you at 8 **o'clock**.*

## octopus

An octopus is a sea animal with eight long arms and a soft body.

## odd number

You cannot put odd numbers into groups of two.

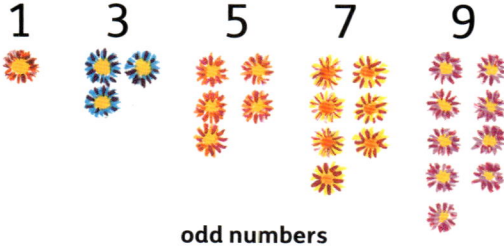

**odd numbers**

## offline

Offline means not connected to the internet.

## offspring

Offspring are the young of an animal.

*A horse's **offspring** is called a foal.*

## oil

Oil is a thick, slippery liquid. It can be burned to keep people warm, or put on machines to help them move easily. Some kinds of oil are used in cooking.

## old

Someone born a long time ago is old. Something is old when it is not new.

 young   old

new          old

## omnivore

An omnivore is an animal that eats plants and meat.

Seagulls are omnivores.

## online

Online means connected to the internet.

## opaque

An object is opaque if you cannot see through it.

*If curtains are **opaque**, you cannot see through them.*

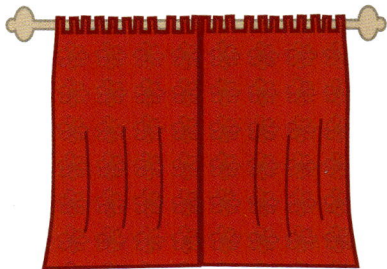

The opposite of opaque is transparent. Look up the word *transparent* on page 96.

## open

To open a computer file or an app means you start it up.

## operation

❶ In maths, add, subtract, multiply and divide are number operations.

*The signs tell you which **operation** to use.*

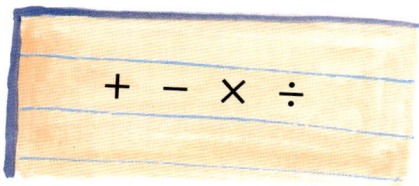

+ − × ÷

❷ In computing, an operation is anything that a computer does, such as a calculation.

*A command tells the computer to carry out an **operation**.*

## opposite

❶ The opposite of something is the thing that is as different from it as possible.

*Big is the **opposite** of small.*

big                     small

❷ If something is opposite something else, it is across from it or facing it.

*Our house is **opposite** the school.*

## order

Order is the way something is set out, one thing after another. You can write numbers and days of the week in order.

10th Monday
11th Tuesday
12th Wednesday

order of days

1 2 3 4 5

order of numbers

## organ

Organs in your body include your brain, heart, lungs, stomach and gut.

*Your skin is the largest **organ** of your body.*

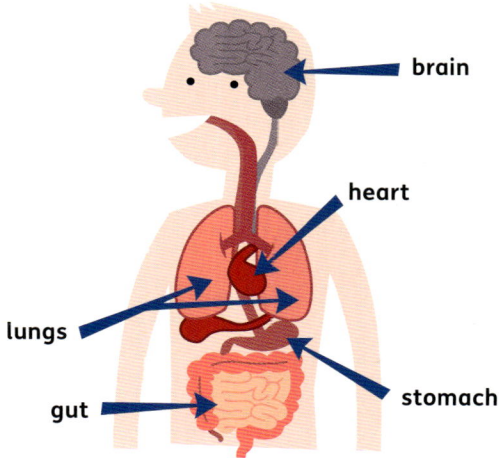

brain

heart

lungs

gut

stomach

## output

Output means taking data from a computer and putting it in a useful form. It might be something that you can see or it might be sound.

Look up the word *data* on page 25.

## oval

An oval is a 2D shape that looks like a squashed circle.

## over

Over means above or on top of.

*The elephant walked **over** the bridge.*

## owe

If you owe money to someone, you have not paid them.

## owl

An owl is a bird with a large, round head and large eyes. Owls hunt small animals at night.

## oxygen

One of the gases in the air is oxygen.

*Animals need **oxygen** to stay alive.*

# Pp

is for **peacock**

## pace
A pace is a step you take when you walk.

*a pace*

## pair
A pair is two of anything.

*a pair of socks*

*a pair of ducks*

## palm
A palm is the distance across your hand below the fingers.

*A **palm** is the same width as four fingers.*

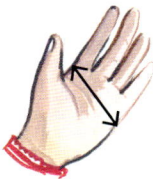

## paper
Paper is made by mashing up wood with water and squashing it into flat sheets.

*We use **paper** to print on, as kitchen roll and as toilet **paper**.*

Daily News

## parachute
A parachute helps to slow the speed of a falling object.

*People and parcels reach the ground safely with **parachutes**.*

## parallel
Parallel lines are the same distance apart and do not cross each other.

***Parallel** lines can be straight or curved.*

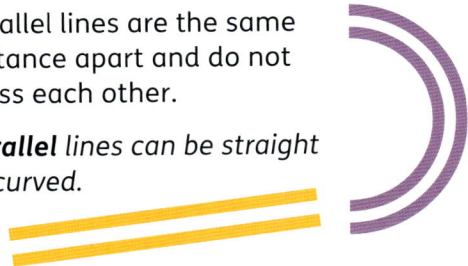

## parallelogram
A parallelogram is a 2D shape with four sides. Its opposite sides are parallel to each other.

## part

You break things into parts. Parts can be equal or unequal.

four equal parts

four unequal parts

## password

A password is a secret word or code that lets you log in to a computer system.

*Can you remember your **password**?*

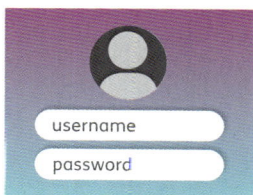

username

password

## pattern

Some patterns have a part that repeats.

a striped pattern

a spotted pattern

## paw

A paw is a mammal's foot that has claws.

## pay

When you pay for something, you give money for it.

*She **pays** for her ice cream.*

## penguin

A penguin is a black and white bird that usually lives in very cold places. Penguins cannot fly, but they are good at swimming.

## pentagon

A pentagon is a 2D shape with five straight sides.

These shapes are all pentagons.

## petal

Petals are the outer part of a flower. They may be brightly coloured.

*Some flowers have more **petals** than others.*

## phishing

Phishing is a way to trick people on the internet by sending them an email that looks real but isn't. It sounds like the word 'fishing'.

## physical property

The physical property of an object is the way it can be seen, touched, heard, smelled or tasted.

## pictogram

A pictogram is a graph that uses pictures.

favourite fruits

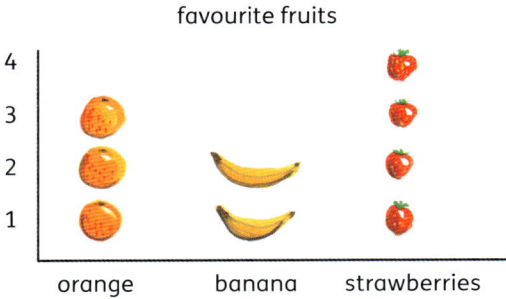

## place value

In a number, the place value tells you what each digit is worth.

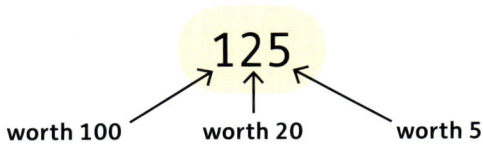

worth 100    worth 20    worth 5

## planet

A planet is any of the worlds in space that move around a star.

*Earth is one of the **planets** that goes around the Sun, which is our closest star.*

## plant

Living things that make their food using sunlight are called plants.

*Trees, grass and bushes are types of **plant**.*

## plastic

Plastic is a material made from oil.

**Plastic can be made into many different shapes.**

## plus

Plus is another name for the adding sign, $+$. It tells you to add.

$2 + 4 = 6$

## point

The points on a shape are the corners.

**A triangle has three points.**

a point

a b c d e f g h
l m n o
Pp
q r s t u v z

## poison

A poison can make you ill or even kill you if you eat or drink it. There are poisonous chemicals in every home.

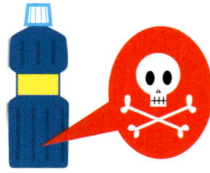

## pole

The poles of a magnet are at the ends.

*The north **pole** of one magnet attracts the south **pole** of another magnet.*

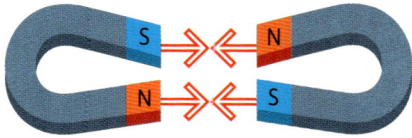

## pollen

Pollen is spread from flower to flower to make new seeds.

*Bees take **pollen** from one flower to another.*

## pollution

Pollution is anything that spoils the environment.

*Plastic can cause **pollution**.*

## polygon

A polygon is any 2D shape with straight sides.

*All these shapes are **polygons**.*

## portal

A portal is like a doorway or a gateway. On your computer, it is a website that has information on a particular subject and links to other websites.

## position

A position word tells you where something is.

up

left

right

in front of

behind

down

## powder

A powder is made of tiny grains of dry material.

*Sugar and flour are **powders**.*

sugar

## prey

Prey animals are ones that are hunted and eaten by other animals.

**The fish is prey for the cat.**

## price

The price is the money you have to pay to buy something.

*The **price** of chips is £2.00.*

## print

When a machine prints words or pictures, it puts them on to paper.

## printer

A printer is a device that makes a copy of a document on paper.

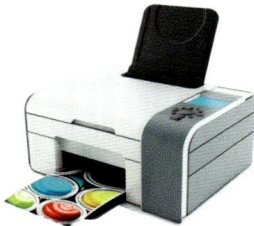

## program

A computer program is a set of instructions. When you run the program, the computer follows the instructions.

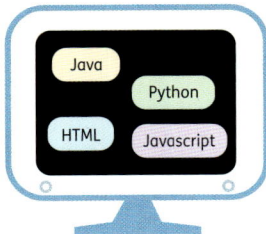

## pupa

A caterpillar makes a pupa. The caterpillar rests inside the pupa as it changes into a flying insect.

Look up the word *caterpillar* on page 17.

## pupil

The dark part of the eye is a hole called the pupil.

*The **pupil** lets light into the eye.*

pupil

## pus

Pus is a thick, yellow liquid that forms in infected cuts and spots.

## pyramid

A pyramid has triangular faces that meet at a point.

pyramids

a b c d e f g h i j k l m n o **Pp** q r s t u v w x y z

# Qq is for **quetzal**

## quarter

When you divide something into quarters, there are four equal parts. You can write a quarter like this $\frac{1}{4}$.

quarters

not quarters

$\frac{1}{4}$ one quarter

$\frac{2}{4}$ two quarters

$\frac{3}{4}$ three quarters

$\frac{4}{4}$ four quarters

## quarter turn

A quarter turn is when you make a quarter of a whole turn.

start        a quarter turn        a half turn

## queen

Insects that live in big groups, such as ants and bees, have queens. The queen lays all the eggs.

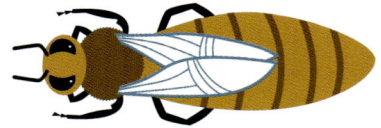

## quick

Quick describes how fast something moves.

quick        quicker        quickest

# R r

is for **rabbit**

## rain

Rain is drops of water falling from clouds.

## rainbow

Rainbows form when sunlight shines through raindrops.

Sunlight is split into many colours when it shines through drops of water.

## rainforest

A rainforest is a large forest in a tropical part of the world, where there is a lot of rain.

## record

When you record something, you write it down or make a copy of it.

## rectangle

A rectangle is a 2D shape that has four straight sides and four right angles.

*All these are **rectangles**.*

A rectangular shape is one that looks like a rectangle.

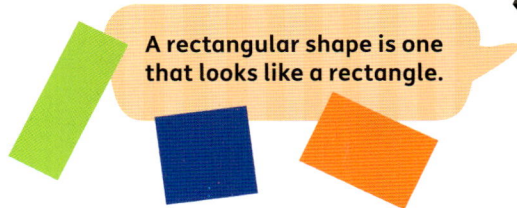

## reflect

Shiny objects reflect light.

## reflection

A reflection is what you see when you look in a mirror.

reflection     mirror

a b c d e f g h i j k l m n o p q **Rr** s t u v w x y z

## reflective symmetry

Reflective symmetry is when one half is the reflection of the other half.

*This flower has **reflective symmetry**.*

## regular shape

All the sides and the angles of a regular shape are the same size.

*All these are **regular** shapes.*

The opposite of regular is irregular. Look up *irregular shape* on page 50.

## remainder

A remainder is what is left after you share something out equally.

*11 shared between 3 leaves a **remainder** of 2.*

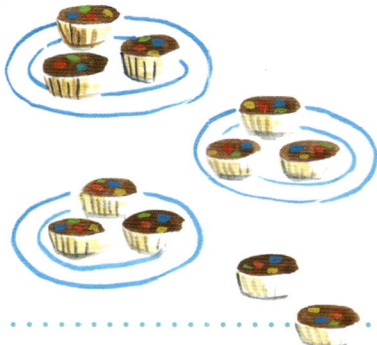

## repeat

When something repeats, it happens again.

*112 **repeats** in this pattern of numbers.*

112112112112112

## repel

Magnets repel when they push each other away.

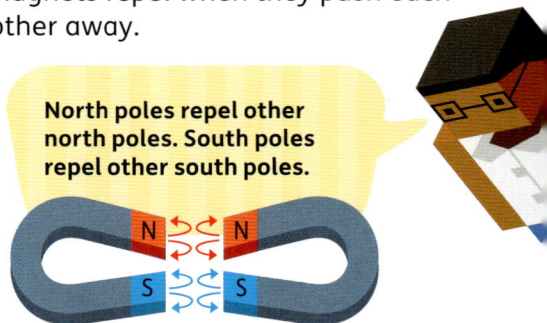

North poles repel other north poles. South poles repel other south poles.

N    N

S    S

## represent

Represent means 'stand for'.
The pictures in a pictogram represent numbers or things.

*Each picture **represents** one animal.*

4
3
2
1

dog    cat    rabbit    goldfish

## reproduce

Living things reproduce when they have babies or make seeds that grow or lay eggs that hatch.

## reptile

Reptiles are animals with dry, scaly skin. They lay eggs with leathery shells.

*Crocodiles and snakes are both **reptiles**.*

## rhinoceros

A rhinoceros is a very large animal with thick skin. It can have one or two horns on its nose. It is called a rhino for short.

## rhombus

A rhombus is a 2D shape with four equal sides. The opposite sides are parallel. When it is turned on its side, it can also be called a diamond.

## rib

Ribs are the bones that protect the organs in your chest.

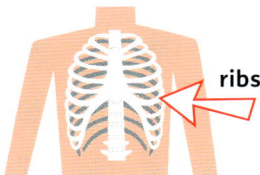

ribs

## right

One side of your body is the right side.

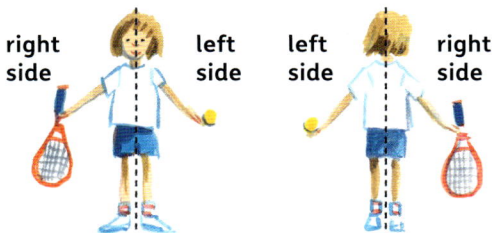

right side    left side    left side    right side

## right angle

A right angle is a quarter of a whole turn.

a whole turn    a quarter turn    a right angle

## robot

A robot is a machine that can move and do jobs. In stories, robots often look a bit like people.

## rock

The Earth is made of hard rock.

## root

Roots hold plants in the ground. Plants take in water through their roots.

*We eat some plant **roots**.*

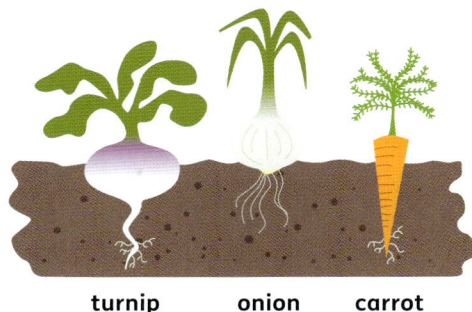

turnip    onion    carrot

## rotate

When you rotate something, you turn it.

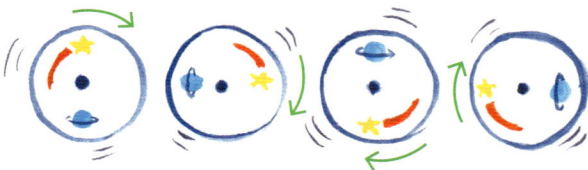

## round

A round shape has curves in it.

round sides

round edges

## row

A row goes across from side to side.

There are four rows in the grid below.

| 1 | 2 | 3 | 4 |
|---|---|---|---|
| 5 | 6 | 7 | 8 |
| 9 | 10 | 11 | 12 |
| 13 | 14 | 15 | 16 |

← a row

## rule

In maths, a rule tells you what to do to change a number.

*The **rule** for this machine is add 2.*

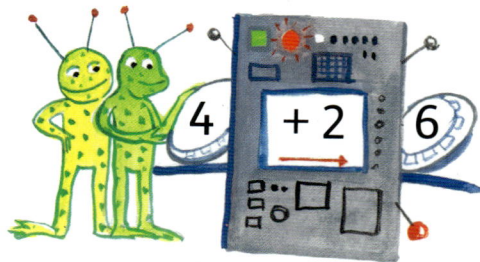

## ruler

You use a ruler to measure and to draw straight lines.

## run

❶ When you run, you use your legs to move quickly.

❷ When you run a computer program, the computer carries out the instructions in the program.

## rust

When iron rusts, it gets a reddish-brown covering.

*Water and air cause iron to **rust**.*

# Ss

is for **swan**

## salt

Salt is powdered rock that we sprinkle on food.

*Salt is also put on roads in winter to melt the snow and ice.*

salt

## save

If you save a computer file, a copy of it is stored in the computer so you can use it again.

**Don't forget to save your work before you log off.**

## scale

A scale is one of the small, thin pieces of hard skin that cover animals like fish and snakes.

scale

## scales

Some scales weigh in grams and some weigh in kilograms.

grams

100 kg

scales

## scanner

A scanner is a machine that makes a copy of text or a picture that can be stored by a computer.

## science

Science is studying things that happen in the world around us in an organized and logical way.

## scientific

Scientific means to do with science.

## screen

A screen is a flat area on a computer, smartphone or tablet that shows an image or data.

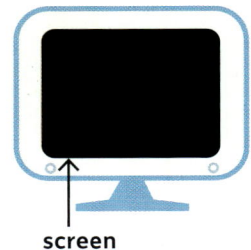

screen

## scroll

Scrolling is moving the pages of a document up or down on a screen.

## sea

The sea is the salt water that covers most of the Earth's surface.

## seal

A seal is a furry animal that lives in the sea and on land. Seals have flippers for swimming.

## search

To search means to try to find something, such as a piece of information. For example, you might search for something in a database or on the internet.

## seashore

Seashore is the land close to the sea.

## season

In Europe, the four seasons are winter, spring, summer and autumn.

Hot countries may have dry and wet seasons.

winter      spring      summer      autumn

## second

A second is a very short time. There are 60 seconds in 1 minute.

*Some watches have a **second** hand.*

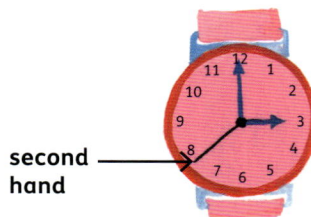

second hand

## seed

Seeds are dry objects from which a new flowering plant will grow.

*These **seeds** will grow into new flowers.*

## seedling

The tiny plant that grows after a seed has sprouted is a seedling.

## select

If you select some text or an image in a computer file, you pick it out by clicking on it.

## sell

When you sell something, you receive money for it.

*The clown **sells** balloons.*

## senses

Our five senses are sight, hearing, touch, smell and taste.

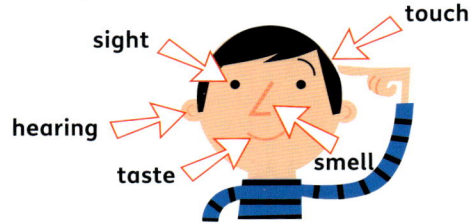

touch

sight

hearing

taste          smell

## sequence

A sequence is a line of numbers. The numbers in a sequence follow a rule.

The rule for this sequence is add 3.

3  6  9  12  15  →

## set

A set is a group of things.

a set of cars

a set of trains

## shadow

The dark area where light is blocked is a shadow.

## shallow

When something is shallow, it is not very deep.

The opposite of shallow is deep. Look up the word *deep* on page 26.

shallow      deep

## shape

A shape can be 2D or 3D.

2D shapes

3D shapes

## share

❶ When you share, you divide things equally.

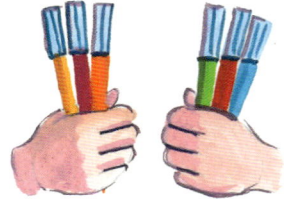

6 shared equally

6 shared unequally

❷ When you share a computer file, photo or data, you send it to someone else.

## shark

A shark is a large fish with lots of sharp teeth.

## sheep

A sheep is an animal that is kept on farms for its wool and meat.

## shell

Shells are the hard outer coverings of snails and some sea animals.

Look up the word *snail* on page 86.

## short

You use short to describe the length of something.

short

shorter

shortest

## sick

Someone who is sick does not feel well.

## sign

A sign is a short way of saying something.

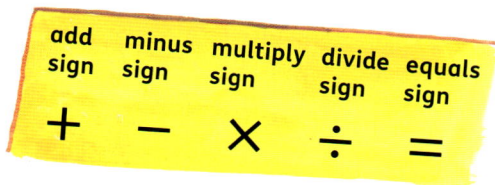

| add sign | minus sign | multiply sign | divide sign | equals sign |
|----------|------------|---------------|-------------|-------------|
| + | − | × | ÷ | = |

## silhouette

A strong shadow made by an object is called a silhouette.

## sink

If something sinks, it goes downwards, usually under water.

## size

You measure something to find out its size.

## skeleton

A skeleton is a frame for the soft parts of the body.

*Your **skeleton** looks like this.*

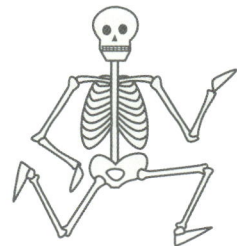

a b c d e f g h i j k l m n o p q r **Ss** t u v w x y z

## skin

Skin is the body's outer covering.

*Rhinoceroses have very thick, folded **skin**.*

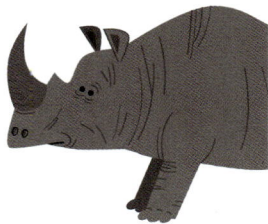

## skull

The skull is the hard case of bone that protects the brain.

*Many animals have a **skull**.*

human skull    horse skull

## sky

The sky is the space above the Earth where you can see the clouds, Sun, Moon and stars.

## slow

You use the word slow when talking about speed and about time.

slow      slower      slowest

## small

You use small when describing the size of things.

small      smaller      smallest

## smartphone

A smartphone is a mobile phone that you can also use as a computer.

Look up *mobile phone* on page 61.

## smart speaker

A smart speaker is a device that can connect to the internet and play sound and music. You can control it using your voice.

## snail

A snail is a small, soft animal that lives inside a shell. Snails move very slowly.

## snake

A snake is a reptile with a long, thin body and no legs.

## snow

Snow is frozen water crystals. Snow is made up of lots of tiny snowflakes.

Did you know that all snowflakes are different shapes?

## social media

Social media is all the websites and apps that people use to communicate with each other on the internet.

## software

Software is another way of saying programs for a computer.

## soil

Soil is a mixture of ground up rock and the remains of dead plants and animals.

## solid

Solid objects keep their shape. Solids can be cut and joined.

*These objects are all **solid**.*

## solid shape

A solid shape has thickness. It is also called a three-dimensional, or 3D, shape.

All these are solid shapes.

## sort

When you sort a set of objects, you put them in groups.

apples

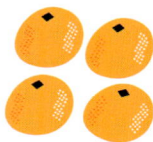

oranges

## sound

Sound is caused by vibrations. You hear sound with your ears.

*When you hit a drum, it vibrates and makes a **sound**.*

## spam

Spam means adverts sent by email that you have not asked for and do not want.

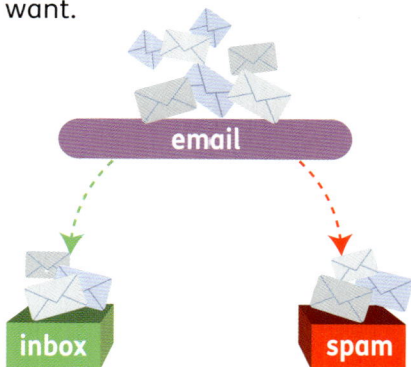

## span

A span is the distance from your little finger to your thumb.

*You stretch out your fingers to make a **span**.*

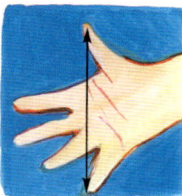

## spawn

Spawn is the eggs of fish or of some other water creatures.

*Frog**spawn** is eggs that look like jelly and are laid by frogs in water.*

## speed

Speed is how quickly something moves or happens.

*The dog ran past at great **speed**.*

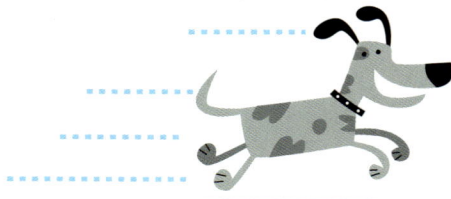

## spend

You spend money when you buy something.

*You **spend** money to buy shopping.*

## sphere

A sphere is perfectly round, like a table tennis ball. It is a 3D shape.

*All these are **spheres**.*

## spider

A spider is a small animal with eight legs. Many spiders make webs to catch insects to eat.

## spine

❶ Your spine is the long row of bones down the middle of your back.

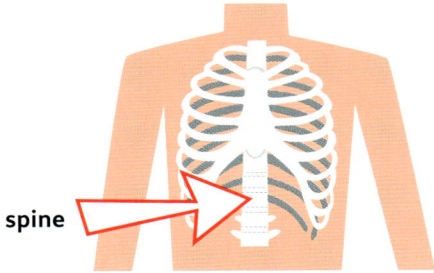

spine

❷ Spines are prickles or thorns on an animal or plant.

*Hedgehogs are covered with* **spines**.

spines

## spreadsheet

A spreadsheet is a computer program that sets out data in a table of rows and columns. The spreadsheet can do calculations.

|   | sport | teams | players |
|---|-------|-------|---------|
| 1 | football | yes | 22 |
| 2 | tennis | no | 2 |
| 3 | rugby | yes | 30 |
| 4 | basketball | yes | 10 |

## spring

❶ Spring is the time of the year when the days get lighter and warmer and plants start to grow.

❷ A spring is a piece of metal that is wound into rings so that it jumps back into shape after it has been squashed.

## square

The four sides of a square are the same size and all the corners are right angles.

*All these are* **squares**.

## squash

When you squash something, you press it hard so that it becomes flat.

*The ball was* **squashed** *by the dog.*

## standard unit

You use standard units when you measure things.

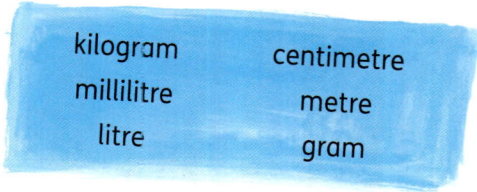

kilogram      centimetre
millilitre      metre
litre      gram

## star

❶ Stars are suns that are so far away they look like tiny bright lights in the night sky.

The Sun is our closest star.

❷ A star is a also a 2D shape that can have different numbers of points.

*All these shapes are **stars**.*

## stem

The stem is the stiff part of a plant that holds the leaves.

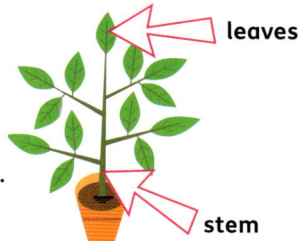

leaves

stem

## step

A step is the distance between your feet when you walk normally.

**a step**

## stomach

Your stomach is the bag into which food goes after you have swallowed it.

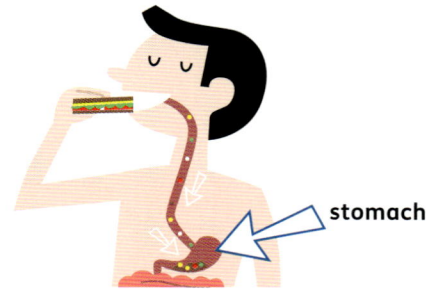

stomach

## stone

A stone is a small piece of rock.

## straight

Something that is straight has no bends or curves in it.

*Draw a **straight** line with the ruler.*

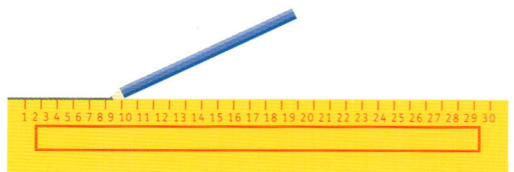

1 2 3 4 5 6 7 8 9 10 11 12 13 14 15 16 17 18 19 20 21 22 23 24 25 26 27 28 29 30

## straight angle

A straight angle is half a whole turn. It is the same as two right angles.

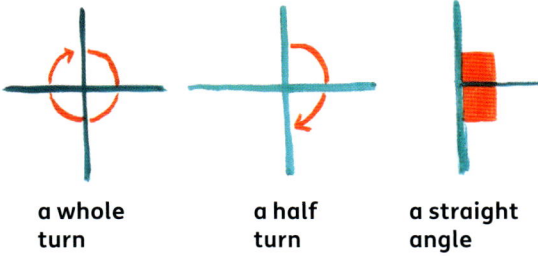

| | | |
|---|---|---|
| a whole turn | a half turn | a straight angle |

## stream

❶ A stream is a small river.

❷ To stream is to watch a video or listen to music while it is downloading from the internet.

## stretch

When an object is pulled and gets longer, it is stretched.

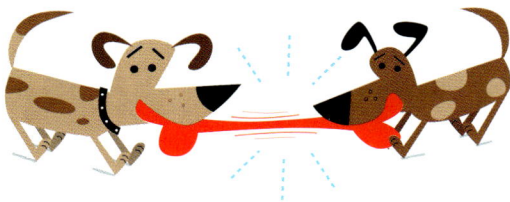

## stride

A stride is the distance between your feet when you take a large step.

a stride

## strong

Objects that cannot be broken easily are strong.

*The bridge is* **strong** *enough to carry the elephant.*

## subtract

When you subtract, you take away.

$$6 - 2 = 4$$

A B C D E F G H I J K L M N O P Q R **Ss** T U V W X Y Z

## subtraction

Subtraction is taking things away. The sign for subtraction is —.

Look up *take away* on page 93.

$$7 - 4 = 3$$

## sum

The sum is the answer you get when you add numbers together.

What is the sum of the numbers below?

The answer is 10.

2          3          5

## summer

Summer is the time of the year when the weather is hot and it stays light for longer in the evenings.

## Sun

The Sun is a huge ball of burning gas. It gives us light and heat.

*The **Sun** is our closest star.*

## survival

Survival means the way something manages to keep on living even when there are dangers.

## sweat

Sweat is the water that leaks out of your skin when you are hot.

***Sweat** cools you down after you have been running.*

## switch

A switch can turn electricity on and off.

*When the **switch** is off, the circuit does not work.*

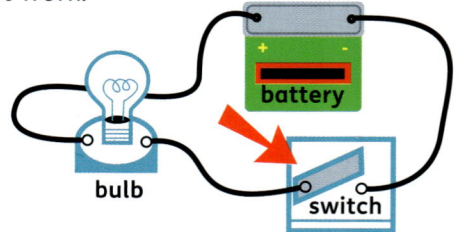

battery

bulb

switch

## symmetrical

One half of a symmetrical shape is a reflection of the other half.

# Tt

**is for tortoise**

## tablet

A tablet is a small, flat computer with a touchscreen.

## tadpole

A tadpole is a tiny animal that lives in water and will turn into a frog or toad.

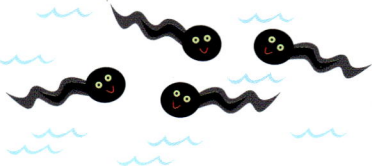

## take away

When you take away, you take one number away from another.

6 take away 4 leaves 2

## tall

You use tall when you talk about the height of things.

tall          taller          tallest

## tally

A tally is a small mark to show how often something happens.

*The **tallies** show that three people ate rolls.*

## tally chart

A tally chart has tallies for different things.

a tally chart

## tape measure

A tape measure can bend and let you measure round things.

*A **tape measure** can be quite long.*

## tears

Tears are water that leaks out of your eyes when you are sad or in pain.

Some people cry when they are very happy!

## teenager

A teenager is someone who is between 13 and 19 years old.

## teen number

A teen number is any number from 13 to 19.

These are the **teen numbers**.

13  14  15  16
17  18  19

## teeth

Teeth are the hard parts in a mouth that are used to chew food.

Lions have big teeth to hold on to their prey.

## telescope

Telescopes are long tubes with special magnifying glasses at each end.

*Telescopes make faraway objects seem much nearer.*

## temperature

Temperature is a measure of how hot something is. You measure temperature in degrees Celsius (°C).

When the temperature is low, it is cold.

When the temperature is high, it is hot.

cold          hot

## ten number

A ten number always ends in 0.

*All these are **ten numbers**.*

10  20  30  40

# text

**❶** Text is words that are written or printed.

**❷** A text is a short written message sent between mobile phones. If you text someone, you send them a text.

*I got a funny **text** from my sister.*

What do you call a lion at the North Pole?
...Lost!

# textile

Textile is a type of material that is used to make fabric or clothes.

Look up the word *fabric* on page 36.

knitted

woven

# text message

A text message is a short written message sent between mobile phones.

# third

When you divide something into thirds, it has three equal parts. You can write a third as $\frac{1}{3}$.

$\frac{1}{3}$ one third

$\frac{2}{3}$ two thirds

$\frac{3}{3}$ three thirds

# three-dimensional

Shapes that are three-dimensional have a length, width and thickness.

*The symbol 3D is short for **three-dimensional**.*

cone

cylinder

cuboid

# throat

Your throat connects your mouth to your stomach and lungs.

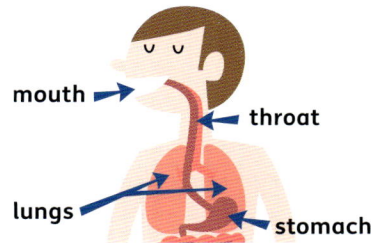

mouth

throat

lungs

stomach

# time

**❶** Time is how long something takes. It is measured in minutes, hours, days and years.

**❷** The time is the hour and minutes when something is happening. You tell the time by looking at a clock.

*What **time** is it now?*

# times

Times is a word for multiply. The times sign is ✕.

4 times 2 is 8

$4 \times 2 = 8$

A F G H I J K L M N O P Q R S **Tt** U V W X Y Z

## times table

You use your times tables when you multiply.

*This is your two times table. Go to page 118 for more times tables.*

$$1 \times 2 = 2$$
$$2 \times 2 = 4$$
$$3 \times 2 = 6$$
$$4 \times 2 = 8$$
$$5 \times 2 = 10$$
$$6 \times 2 = 12$$
$$7 \times 2 = 14$$
$$8 \times 2 = 16$$
$$9 \times 2 = 18$$
$$10 \times 2 = 20$$

## toddler

A toddler is a young child who is just beginning to walk.

## toolbar

A toolbar is the area at the top of a computer screen that has icons on it that represent different apps, files or tasks.

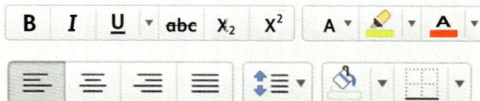

## total

You find out the total when you add.

*What is the total of these numbers below?*

The total is 10.

2          3          5

## touchscreen

A touchscreen is a type of screen that you touch to select or run a program.

## transparent

Transparent objects are see-through.

## tree

Trees are large, woody plants with a trunk.

*Evergreen **trees** keep their leaves all year round. Deciduous **trees** lose their leaves in winter.*

trunk

evergreen tree          deciduous tree

## triangle

A triangle is a 2D shape with three straight sides.

*All these are **triangles**.*

## trunk

❶ The trunk on a tree is the thick stem that grows up out of the ground.

trunk

❷ An elephant's trunk is its long nose.

trunk

## tummy

Your tummy is under your chest. Another word for tummy is abdomen.

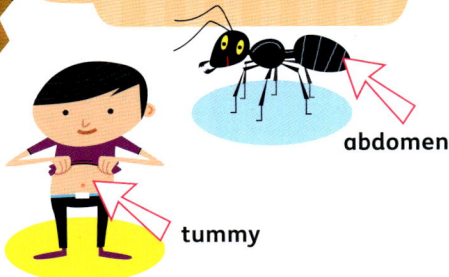

An insect's abdomen is the end part of its body.

abdomen

tummy

## TV

TV stands for television. A television is a machine that receives pictures and sound so that people can watch TV programmes.

## twice

Twice means two times.

Twice 3 is 6.

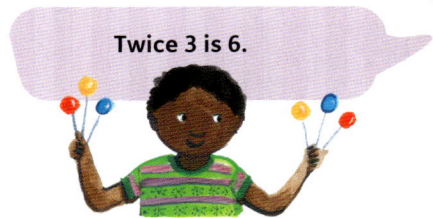

## twist

❶ When you twist something, you turn it round.

*She **twisted** the lid off the jar.*

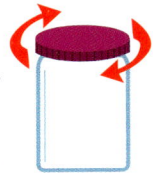

❷ When you twist things together, you turn them round each other so that they become fixed together.

*Electrical wires are often **twisted** together.*

## two-dimensional

Shapes that are two-dimensional have a length and width but no thickness.

*The symbol 2D is short for **two-dimensional**.*

square

triangle

hexagon

# Uu
## is for **umbrella bird**

## under
Under means below.

*The water flows **under** the bridge.*

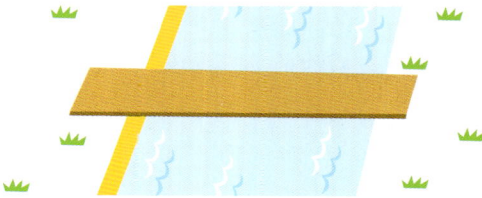

## unequal
If two things are unequal, they are not the same size or worth.

**equal parts**          **unequal parts**

## unit
❶ You measure things in units.

*Metres are **units** used to measure length.*

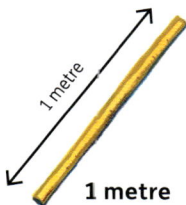  

**1 metre**     **1 kilogram**     **1 litre**

❷ Units is also another name for ones.

*There are 5 **units** in the number 125.*

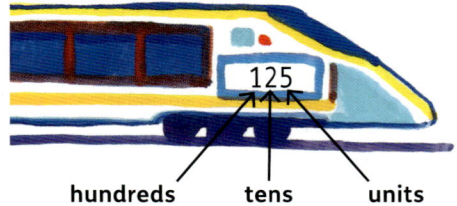

hundreds      tens      units

## update
❶ To update something is to bring it up to date. You sometimes get a message on your smartphone asking if you want to update the software.

❷ An update is a change made by updating something.

## urine
Urine is the waste water we pass out of our bodies.

## username
A username is the name you use when you log in to a website or computer system.

Look up the word *password* on page 72.

username

password

A B C D E F G H I J K L M N O P Q R S T Uu V W X Y Z

# Vv
## is for **vulture**

## vaccination
A vaccination is an injection that stops you getting an illness.

## vegetable
A vegetable is part of a plant that is used as food.

## vein
Veins carry blood around the body.

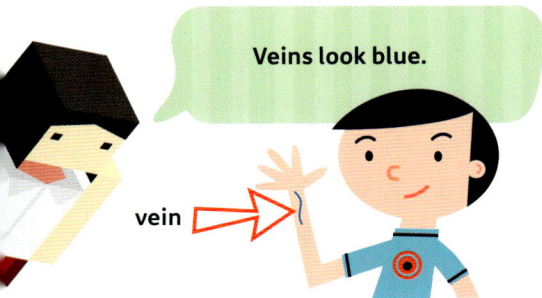

Veins look blue.

vein

## Venn diagram
You use a Venn diagram to sort things into groups.

triangles          not triangles

## vertex
A vertex is the point of a shape. The plural of vertex is vertices.

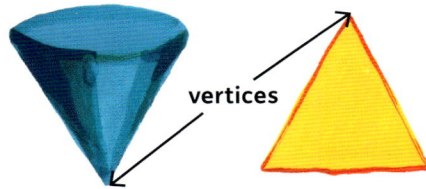

vertices

## vibrate
When an object vibrates, it moves very quickly backwards and forwards.

## video
A video is a film or programme that has been recorded. You can watch it on a phone or computer.

## video game

Video games are played on a computer. There are many types of video game. Some games have puzzles and some are adventures that you can take part in.

A video game is also called a computer game.

## virus

❶ Viruses are tiny living things that can make us ill.

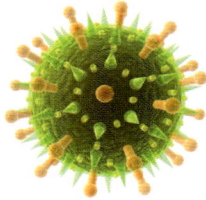

❷ A virus is also a type of computer program that damages the data in computer files.

## volume

❶ Very noisy things have a high sound volume.

❷ Volume is the amount of space an object takes up or how much it holds.

*Another word for **volume** is capacity.*

## vote

When you vote, you choose.

*Three children **vote** for the colour red.*

favourite colour
red ✓ ✓ ✓
green ✓
blue ✓ ✓

## VR

VR stands for virtual reality. It means images and sounds that are made by a computer which feel like real life. You can be part of a VR scene by wearing special equipment.

# Ww

is for **walrus**

## warm-blooded

Birds and mammals are warm-blooded. They keep their body warmer than the air around them.

Hair or feathers help mammals and birds to keep warm.

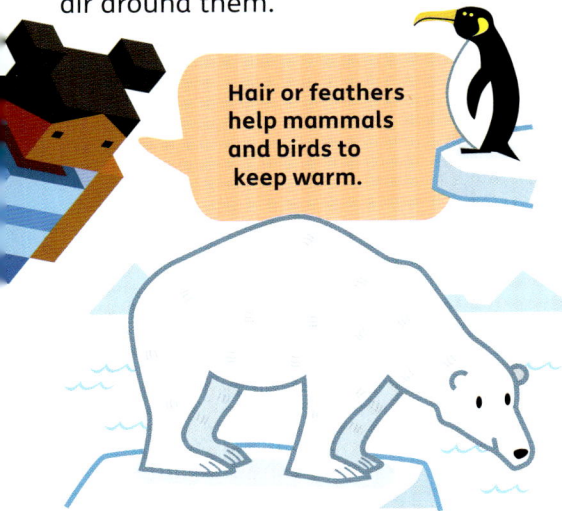

## water

Water is a liquid at room temperature. It is essential for all living things.

*Water can be in solid, liquid or gas form.*

solid    liquid    gas

## waterproof

Waterproof materials do not let water through them.

## weather

The weather is what it is like outside, for example whether the sun is shining or it is rainy or windy.

## web

❶ A web is a thin, sticky net made by a spider to catch insects.

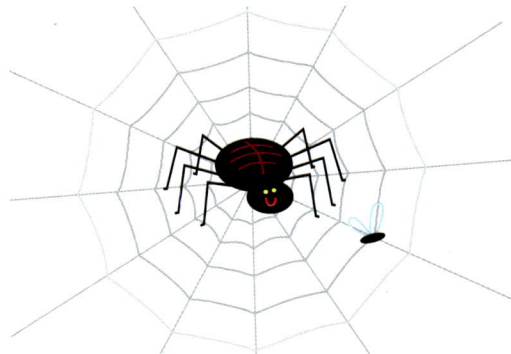

❷ The web is another name for the World Wide Web.

## website

A website is a place on the internet where you can get information.

## weed

Weeds are plants that we don't want.

*Nettles and dandelions are common* **weeds**.

## week

A week has 7 days.

There are 52 weeks in a year.

Monday

Tuesday

Wednesday

Thursday

Friday

Saturday

Sunday

## weekend

The weekend days are Saturday and Sunday.

*Let's have a picnic this* **weekend**.

## weigh

You weigh something to find out how heavy it is.

*You can* **weigh** *yourself.*

## weight

❶ Weight is how heavy something is. You measure weight or mass in grams and kilograms.

Look up the word *mass* on page 58.

❷ You can use weights to find out how heavy things are.

## whole

A whole shape is not broken into parts.

whole          half          quarter

## whole number

A whole number is not a fraction.

Look up the word *fraction* on page 40.

$\frac{1}{2}$ is a fraction

2 is a whole number

$1\frac{1}{2}$ is a whole number and a fraction

## whole turn

A whole turn is a complete turn. It is the same as four right angles.

a whole turn

## wide

When something is wide, its sides are far apart.

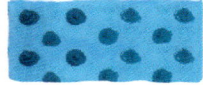

wide          wider          widest

## width

Width is the distance across something.

the width of a river

## Wi-Fi™

Wi-Fi™ is a way that devices can communicate or connect to the internet without wires.

*Do you have **Wi-Fi™** here?*

## wing

Wings help an animal to fly. Aeroplanes also have wings to help them fly.

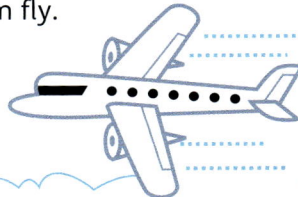

## winter

Winter is the time of the year when the weather is cold and it gets dark early in the evenings.

## wire

Wires are long, thin strands of metal. Sometimes, wires are covered in plastic or rubber.

*Wire is used to make many things.*

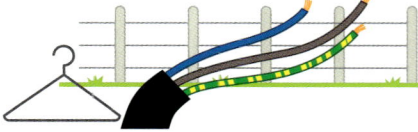

## wood

Wood is the hard material that trees are made of. People burn wood as fuel or use it to make things.

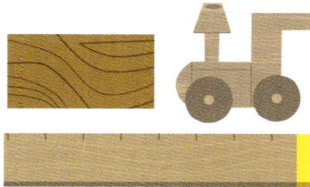

## woodland

A woodland is an area of land where a lot of trees grow.

## woodlice

Woodlice are small creatures with seven pairs of legs and no wings. They live in damp wood or soil.

## wool

Wool is the thick, soft hair that covers sheep. It is used for making clothes.

wool

## world

The world is the Earth and everything on it.

## World Wide Web

The World Wide Web is made up of all the websites in the world. They are connected through the internet.

**Look up the word *internet* on page 50.**

# X x
## is for **X-ray**

## X

You will see the letter X written on some clock faces. It means 10.

Some clocks have numerals instead of numbers. Look up the word *numeral* on page 66.

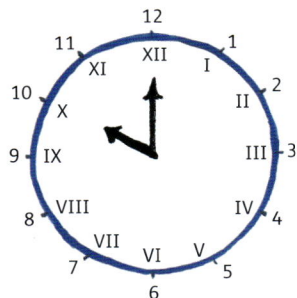

## X-ray

X-rays are rays that can pass through flesh but not bone. You cannot see X-rays.

We use X-rays to take pictures of broken bones.

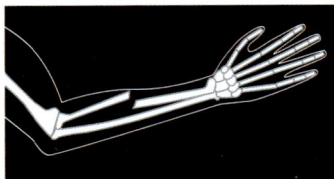

# Y y
## is for **yak**

## year

A year is a measure of time. There are 12 months in a year.

Go to page 116 to learn the 12 months of the year.

## yolk

The yolk is the yellow part of an egg.

The yolk is a food store for the chick inside the egg.

## young

Someone born a short time ago is young.

**young**        **younger**        **youngest**

a b c d e f g h l m q r s t u v w **Xx** **Yy** z

# Zz

## is for **zebra**

### zero

Zero is another word for nothing or nought.

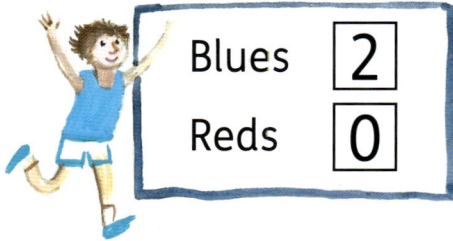

Blues 2
Reds 0

### zoo

A zoo is a place where many animals are kept.

When you go to the zoo, you can see lots of different animals from all around the world.

# Maths doing words

| | | |
|---|---|---|
| add | find | roll |
| arrange | finish | round to |
| build | fold | shade |
| carry on | group | share |
| check | guess | slide |
| choose | match | sort |
| collect | measure | split |
| colour | pick out | take |
| compare | place | tick |
| complete | point to | trace |
| continue | predict | turn |
| copy | present | use |
| count | put in order | weigh |
| cross | record | work out |
| fill in | ring | |

# Science doing words

| | | |
|---|---|---|
| boil | feel | melt |
| burn | filter | mix |
| change | float | observe |
| check | fly | plan |
| classify | freeze | predict |
| collect | graph | record |
| compare | grow | repeat |
| cool | guess | sieve |
| count | hear | smell |
| dissolve | heat | sort |
| draw | listen | test |
| experiment | look | touch |
| explain | measure | weigh |

# Computing doing words

| | | |
|---|---|---|
| browse | drag | program |
| click | edit | run |
| code | email | save |
| connect | game | scan |
| control | highlight | scroll |
| copy | instruct | search |
| create | log in | select |
| cut | message | share |
| debug | open | stream |
| delete | operate | type |
| double-click | paste | update |
| download | print | upload |

# Maths apparatus

abacus
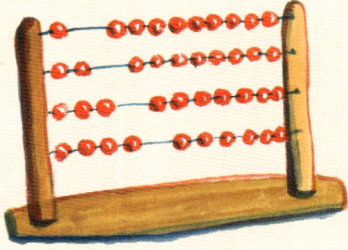

digit cards

balance

dominoes

calculator

equalizer

dice

geoboard
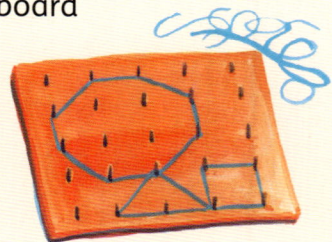

**interlocking cubes**

**number rods**

**measuring jug**

**peg board**

**number cards**

**place value apparatus**

**number fan**

**timer**

# Science equipment

computer
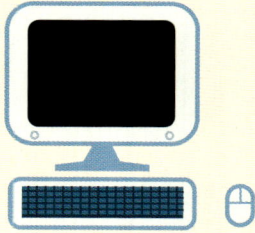

magnifying glass

electrical equipment
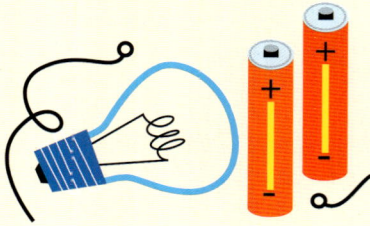

measuring jugs
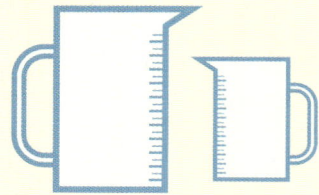

kitchen scales

microscope

magnets

pooter

## sieves, filters and funnels

## tape measure, metre rule, ruler

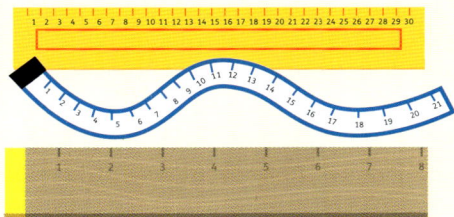

## specimen bottle

## thermometers

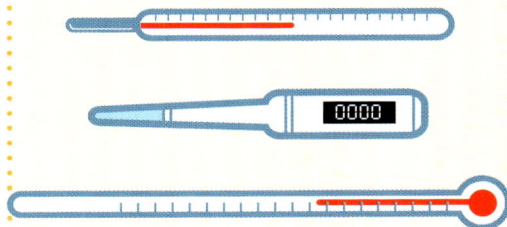

## spring balance

## torches

## stopwatch

## weighing scales

# Computing equipment

computer

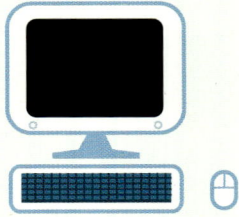

laptop

console

memory card

disk

memory stick

keyboard

monitor

mouse

smart speaker

printer

speaker

scanner

tablet

smartphone

tower computer

# Days of the week

Monday
Tuesday
Wednesday
Thursday
Friday
**Saturday**
**Sunday** } The weekend

Monday
Tuesday
Wednesday
Thursday
Friday
Saturday
Sunday

# Months of the year

*In a leap year, there are 29 days in February. A leap year happens every four years.

| | |
|---|---|
| January | 31 days |
| February* | 28 days |
| March | 31 days |
| April | 30 days |
| May | 31 days |
| June | 30 days |
| July | 31 days |
| August | 31 days |
| September | 30 days |
| October | 31 days |
| November | 30 days |
| December | 31 days |

# Time words

morning　　afternoon　　evening　　day　　night

# Numbers

| | | | | | |
|---|---|---|---|---|---|
| 0 | zero | 0 | zero | 0 | zero |
| 1 | one | 10 | ten | 1,000 | one thousand |
| 2 | two | 20 | twenty | 2,000 | two thousand |
| 3 | three | 30 | thirty | 3,000 | three thousand |
| 4 | four | 40 | forty | 4,000 | four thousand |
| 5 | five | 50 | fifty | 5,000 | five thousand |
| 6 | six | 60 | sixty | 6,000 | six thousand |
| 7 | seven | 70 | seventy | 7,000 | seven thousand |
| 8 | eight | 80 | eighty | 8,000 | eight thousand |
| 9 | nine | 90 | ninety | 9,000 | nine thousand |
| 10 | ten | 100 | hundred | | |
| 11 | eleven | 200 | two hundred | 1st | first |
| 12 | twelve | 300 | three hundred | 2nd | second |
| 13 | thirteen | 400 | four hundred | 3rd | third |
| 14 | fourteen | 500 | five hundred | 4th | fourth |
| 15 | fifteen | 600 | six hundred | 5th | fifth |
| 16 | sixteen | 700 | seven hundred | 6th | sixth |
| 17 | seventeen | 800 | eight hundred | 7th | seventh |
| 18 | eighteen | 900 | nine hundred | 8th | eighth |
| 19 | nineteen | | | 9th | ninth |
| 20 | twenty | | | 10th | tenth |

1st  first     2nd  second     3rd  third     4th  fourth     5th  fifth

# Times tables

## 2 times table

| | | | | |
|---|---|---|---|---|
| 1 | × | 2 | = | 2 |
| 2 | × | 2 | = | 4 |
| 3 | × | 2 | = | 6 |
| 4 | × | 2 | = | 8 |
| 5 | × | 2 | = | 10 |
| 6 | × | 2 | = | 12 |
| 7 | × | 2 | = | 14 |
| 8 | × | 2 | = | 16 |
| 9 | × | 2 | = | 18 |
| 10 | × | 2 | = | 20 |
| 11 | × | 2 | = | 22 |
| 12 | × | 2 | = | 24 |

## 5 times table

| | | | | |
|---|---|---|---|---|
| 1 | × | 5 | = | 5 |
| 2 | × | 5 | = | 10 |
| 3 | × | 5 | = | 15 |
| 4 | × | 5 | = | 20 |
| 5 | × | 5 | = | 25 |
| 6 | × | 5 | = | 30 |
| 7 | × | 5 | = | 35 |
| 8 | × | 5 | = | 40 |
| 9 | × | 5 | = | 45 |
| 10 | × | 5 | = | 50 |
| 11 | × | 5 | = | 55 |
| 12 | × | 5 | = | 60 |

## 3 times table

| | | | | |
|---|---|---|---|---|
| 1 | × | 3 | = | 3 |
| 2 | × | 3 | = | 6 |
| 3 | × | 3 | = | 9 |
| 4 | × | 3 | = | 12 |
| 5 | × | 3 | = | 15 |
| 6 | × | 3 | = | 18 |
| 7 | × | 3 | = | 21 |
| 8 | × | 3 | = | 24 |
| 9 | × | 3 | = | 27 |
| 10 | × | 3 | = | 30 |
| 11 | × | 3 | = | 33 |
| 12 | × | 3 | = | 36 |

## 6 times table

| | | | | |
|---|---|---|---|---|
| 1 | × | 6 | = | 6 |
| 2 | × | 6 | = | 12 |
| 3 | × | 6 | = | 18 |
| 4 | × | 6 | = | 24 |
| 5 | × | 6 | = | 30 |
| 6 | × | 6 | = | 36 |
| 7 | × | 6 | = | 42 |
| 8 | × | 6 | = | 48 |
| 9 | × | 6 | = | 54 |
| 10 | × | 6 | = | 60 |
| 11 | × | 6 | = | 66 |
| 12 | × | 6 | = | 72 |

## 4 times table

| | | | | |
|---|---|---|---|---|
| 1 | × | 4 | = | 4 |
| 2 | × | 4 | = | 8 |
| 3 | × | 4 | = | 12 |
| 4 | × | 4 | = | 16 |
| 5 | × | 4 | = | 20 |
| 6 | × | 4 | = | 24 |
| 7 | × | 4 | = | 28 |
| 8 | × | 4 | = | 32 |
| 9 | × | 4 | = | 36 |
| 10 | × | 4 | = | 40 |
| 11 | × | 4 | = | 44 |
| 12 | × | 4 | = | 48 |

## 7 times table

| | | | | |
|---|---|---|---|---|
| 1 | × | 7 | = | 7 |
| 2 | × | 7 | = | 14 |
| 3 | × | 7 | = | 21 |
| 4 | × | 7 | = | 28 |
| 5 | × | 7 | = | 35 |
| 6 | × | 7 | = | 42 |
| 7 | × | 7 | = | 49 |
| 8 | × | 7 | = | 56 |
| 9 | × | 7 | = | 63 |
| 10 | × | 7 | = | 70 |
| 11 | × | 7 | = | 77 |
| 12 | × | 7 | = | 84 |

## 8 times table

| | | | |
|---|---|---|---|
| 1 | × 8 | = | 8 |
| 2 | × 8 | = | 16 |
| 3 | × 8 | = | 24 |
| 4 | × 8 | = | 32 |
| 5 | × 8 | = | 40 |
| 6 | × 8 | = | 48 |
| 7 | × 8 | = | 56 |
| 8 | × 8 | = | 64 |
| 9 | × 8 | = | 72 |
| 10 | × 8 | = | 80 |
| 11 | × 8 | = | 88 |
| 12 | × 8 | = | 96 |

## 11 times table

| | | | |
|---|---|---|---|
| 1 | × 11 | = | 11 |
| 2 | × 11 | = | 22 |
| 3 | × 11 | = | 33 |
| 4 | × 11 | = | 44 |
| 5 | × 11 | = | 55 |
| 6 | × 11 | = | 66 |
| 7 | × 11 | = | 77 |
| 8 | × 11 | = | 88 |
| 9 | × 11 | = | 99 |
| 10 | × 11 | = | 110 |
| 11 | × 11 | = | 121 |
| 12 | × 11 | = | 132 |

## 9 times table

| | | | |
|---|---|---|---|
| 1 | × 9 | = | 9 |
| 2 | × 9 | = | 18 |
| 3 | × 9 | = | 27 |
| 4 | × 9 | = | 36 |
| 5 | × 9 | = | 45 |
| 6 | × 9 | = | 54 |
| 7 | × 9 | = | 63 |
| 8 | × 9 | = | 72 |
| 9 | × 9 | = | 81 |
| 10 | × 9 | = | 90 |
| 11 | × 9 | = | 99 |
| 12 | × 9 | = | 108 |

## 12 times table

| | | | |
|---|---|---|---|
| 1 | × 12 | = | 12 |
| 2 | × 12 | = | 24 |
| 3 | × 12 | = | 36 |
| 4 | × 12 | = | 48 |
| 5 | × 12 | = | 60 |
| 6 | × 12 | = | 72 |
| 7 | × 12 | = | 84 |
| 8 | × 12 | = | 96 |
| 9 | × 12 | = | 108 |
| 10 | × 12 | = | 120 |
| 11 | × 12 | = | 132 |
| 12 | × 12 | = | 144 |

## 10 times table

| | | | |
|---|---|---|---|
| 1 | × 10 | = | 10 |
| 2 | × 10 | = | 20 |
| 3 | × 10 | = | 30 |
| 4 | × 10 | = | 40 |
| 5 | × 10 | = | 50 |
| 6 | × 10 | = | 60 |
| 7 | × 10 | = | 70 |
| 8 | × 10 | = | 80 |
| 9 | × 10 | = | 90 |
| 10 | × 10 | = | 100 |
| 11 | × 10 | = | 110 |
| 12 | × 10 | = | 120 |

Did you know that multiples of 2, 4 and 8 are all even numbers?

Remember that multiples of 5 will always end with 5 or 0.

# Shapes

## 2D

 semicircle

 circle

 hexagon

 rectangle

 parallelogram

 oval

 pentagon

 triangle

 kite

 square

 rhombus

 octagon

 diamond

## 3D

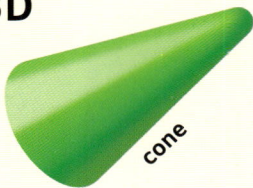 cone

 cube

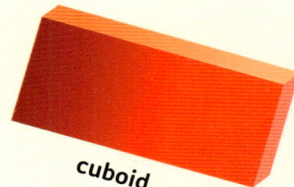 cuboid

 pyramid

 cylinder

 sphere